BROKENHEARTE

Encouraging Stories of Faithfulness, Healing, and Hope in the Midst of Miscarriage and Loss

———

A CRAVING GOD MINISTRIES
DEVOTIONAL COMPLIED BY

HEATHER SHIPLEY

DEDICATION

To all of the precious babies in Heaven, dearly loved and thought of often by their families here on Earth.

And to the mothers (and fathers) who carry these precious ones in their hearts always. May you find healing, community, and hope through faith.

.

CONTENTS

INTRODUCTION
HEATHER'S STORY

I no longer believe in coincidence, but know that in all circumstances God creates purpose. His plan is greater, even when we don't understand it.

They say that one in four women experience the loss of pregnancy through miscarriage, and on October 15, 2015 (National Pregnancy and Infant Loss Remembrance Day), I personally experienced this tragedy for the first time. I was so excited. *My* timeline. *My* perfect plan. My husband and I had just celebrated our fifth wedding anniversary, settled into good jobs, and found a church we could call home. It was time to expand our family.

I started a fall semester small group, and the very first night during a *tell us something no one knows about you* icebreaker I blurted out, "I'M PREGNANT!" I couldn't believe I had shared the news so early. I'm pretty sure I had just peed on a stick that day! Later, I told my closest high school girlfriends, and they revealed that they were pregnant too. (I promise we didn't plan it!) Four friends pregnant at the same time, how exciting! The ultrasound came, but this time the news wasn't as sweet. Things didn't look right. Perhaps the dates were off? In my heart I knew they couldn't be.

Because of my miscarriage, relationships have been rekindled and restored. Not just with family and friends, but also with the version of myself I had almost forgotten. Above all else, my relationship with the Lord was forever transformed. Out of the ashes ministry, passion, and purpose were born.

I am one in four. I no longer believe in coincidence, but know that in all circumstances God creates purpose. His plan is greater, even when we don't understand it.

The exact week I write this would have been the one-year anniversary of my due date. While I would love to be holding a precious one-year-old in my arms, I sit here staring at a rainbow outside my window, so very thankful for the treasures God has provided through the trial.

Women who have or are experiencing miscarriage belong to an often-silent community. It is something not commonly or openly talked about, but I firmly believe there is power in sharing an experience such as this. Not only for self-healing, but in finding purpose through helping others.

The one thing, besides God's Word, that helped me after experiencing miscarriage, was hearing stories of faithfulness, healing, and hope. I knew God had given me a purpose to give others a voice. My prayer exactly one year ago was that "God would use each of us as vessels for His work and glory." I continue to pray that this book and the heart-felt testimonies within will help others find healing and lead them and those around them closer to God, expanding His everlasting Kingdom and giving Him all the glory forever.

"For I know the plans I have for you," declares the Lord, "plans to prosper you and not to harm you, plans to give you hope and a future" (Jeremiah 29:11).

BROKENHEARTED HOPE

CHAPTER 1: NO SECRET TO KEEP
You're Not Alone

---

*God had a plan for me all along. He knew
I needed these connections and perhaps He
knew that they needed me too.*

Amber's Story

In April of 2011, my life changed forever when I found out I was pregnant. My husband and I had previously decided that we'd stop using birth control and just see what happened. It took maybe two weeks and boom, I was pregnant. We were elated! I surprised him with the news in a cheesy way, of course. After that, we decided to tell our parents and one close friend each. I was still in complete shock that it took no time to get pregnant, and couldn't stop thinking about how fortunate I was. I knew it was a little premature, but I decided to go buy a couple of onesies just so that it seemed a little more real.

I was six weeks pregnant when we went to my hometown to tell my parents. I had wrapped a couple of baby toys in a gift bag for them as a present and way to announce it. I videoed their reaction. It was such a joyful and exciting time.

The next week I went to the bathroom at work and noticed some blood in my urine. I immediately took to Google (which is always a bad idea). After reading horror stories, I called my doctor's office and told them what was happening. I then remembered that the first time we went for our official visit they told me that they couldn't see a whole lot on the ultrasound, but that was normal given how early it was. After remembering that I panicked even more. They assured me over the phone that this blood could be completely normal, but we could come in first thing the next day to check things out.

Great, now I had the whole night to stress! The blood never got any worse, and actually stopped, so I was relieved. The next morning the blood came again, and it came with a vengeance. At that point I knew in my heart what was happening. I was having a miscarriage. I told my husband I knew that's what it was and that I didn't think he needed to take off work to come with me. I honestly didn't want him there because I felt like this was somehow my fault and I was feeling guilty. I was ashamed and I didn't want anyone to know what was happening. I was so glad we decided to tell so few people; less people I had to own up to in my mind. I immediately deleted all of the videos from my phone of our parents finding out.

At the doctor's office I kept playing out the words he was going to tell me in my head so it would hopefully be less of a shock. In my mind my response would be "Ok, thank you.

What do we do now?" with a very professional, calm attitude. The actual conversation was a little different.

"You are having a miscarriage Mrs. C." I immediately broke down and began sobbing uncontrollably. At that point in time I wished my husband *had* been there. Why was I such an idiot to think I could do this alone? My doctor stepped right in, wrapped his arms around me, and told me it would be okay. He was so great and understanding. I'll never forget it.

I'll also never forget the next thing he said: "Do not keep this a secret. You need to talk about it. It's more common than you realize and it's not your fault." I surely thought he had lost his mind. This was my fault. I stressed out too much, I didn't eat the right thing, and I must have done something to deserve this. I nodded my head in agreement while internally swearing I would bear this burden and not talk to anyone about it. I was so embarrassed and I feared the looks and judgment I would receive if I told anyone.

This internal anguish went on for a while. I put on a fake smile with friends and joked around with co-workers, although I felt completely deflated. I started playing the blame game. Why did God allow this to happen to me? Why this, why that? Wasn't I doing at least something right to deserve a baby?

About a month after the miscarriage, the Lord started working in me. I literally woke up one morning yearning to talk to someone about my experience. I wasn't sure how to just 'find' these other people that this had happened to, even though my doctor said there were a lot out there. I realized that was the problem. They were out there, but no one was talking about it, so none of us knew of each other.

After you're married for so long the general question becomes "So when are you going to have kids?" This became my intro into a difficult but necessary conversation. I decided to start telling people the truth when they asked this question. My response became "Well, we are definitely trying but I did have a miscarriage recently." I immediately followed it up with a "Don't feel bad!" and told them that it was actually helping me being able to talk about it. Everyone was so understanding. I started getting responses like "Wow, I've had one too," or "I've actually had four."

I found that so many of my friends and acquaintances had been through the exact same thing. I slowly started to develop a network of friends that I could talk to about the raw emotions I was feeling through this experience. God had a plan for me all along. He knew I needed these connections, and perhaps He knew that they needed me too.

We did end up having a little boy, and the journey was a tough one with a lot of pain and tears. I still talk about my miscarriage to anyone that will listen because I feel like it's something that should not be shamed or hidden. I try to encourage others to share their stories to prevent them from going to the dark place I was in for so long. God is using my story and His Will is perfect.

HALEY'S STORY

Until now, I've never spoken publicly about my pregnancy losses. The months immediately following my miscarriages were lonely ones. I pretended the first one didn't happen because the reality was too painful. After my second miscarriage, I reached out to a few family members and close friends to tell them what happened. If I'm honest, I probably wouldn't have told a majority of them if it hadn't been for already sharing the news of my pregnancy.

Many of them were experiencing such joyful times in their lives: engagements, weddings, pregnancies, and births of their own children; and I was mourning the loss of mine. I didn't want to be a "Debbie Downer." I didn't want to be the person that nobody wanted to be around because I dampened the celebratory mood.

On the other hand, I also knew there were people who were walking through extremely challenging seasons in their lives. I didn't want to burden them with my problems. It didn't seem right to call and say, "Hey, I'm sorry, I know you just lost your dad, but can we talk about my miscarriage?" Surely they would hang up on me thinking I was inconsiderate.

It didn't help that a few responses I received could have gone in a book of "What Not to Say to Women Experiencing Miscarriage." I knew they had no idea how badly their words stung, and I have no doubt that their intentions were pure. They were merely trying to speak words of comfort in my time of despair.

Nevertheless, after hearing a few responses such as, "Everything happens for a reason," and "Thank goodness it happened early so you didn't get too attached," it seemed easier to go silent. It only confirmed what I already thought in my mind: there was something wrong with me, and I was on my own to figure it out.

My fear of rejection was a self-created prison. How do you crack your heart wide open and share what's deep inside without being especially sensitive to subjecting yourself to judgment, condemnation, or pity? Self-imposed or not, prisons have one job: to hold prisoners. The walls I put up protected me from the pain of rejection and from experiencing more pain from the well-meaning words of others. I simply stopped sharing to avoid the vulnerability.

I was very much alone in trying to sort out all the fears and feelings of inadequacy that accompanied my second pregnancy loss. Was I being punished? Did God think I would be a bad mother? Did I do something wrong during my pregnancies? Is this my fault? Do I deserve this? The questions haunted me every night, and I had no one to share my fears with. You see, those walls kept a lot of good out as well.

We humans crave connection for a reason. The Lord created us this way with a purpose. We need each other. This is why God uses us to help each other! We come full circle when we use our experiences to help others. This is by divine design!

As more time has passed since my miscarriages, I have become more aware of a trend that gnaws at me. When people lose a loved one: a parent, sibling, grandparent, or child, it's shared with as many people as possible so the church and other friends can rally around them. We show them love by sending flowers and cards, offering to babysit, bringing meals, and covering them in prayer.

My hope is that by increasing awareness of pregnancy loss, women and men walking through this pain will feel more comfortable talking openly about it, and the church, their friends, and family will respond just like they would if the couple had lost a family member. That there would be no more suffering in silence.

As I write this contribution, I am saying a prayer. I know how badly people are suffering this very moment because of this tragedy, and I know they are desperately seeking connection with others who understand their pain. I pray that you know that you are immeasurably loved by your heavenly Father and created with mighty purpose. I pray that you will free yourself from self-imposed prisons and tear down any walls you've built around your heart. There's no need to build walls and imprison yourself because you have done nothing wrong! I pray you experience comfort, perfect peace that surpasses understanding, and complete healing of your heart.

BETH'S STORY

When you experience a failed pregnancy you are inducted into a club. As you share, sisters come forward to share their stories too. You start to learn how many members are in this club, and it's startling.

I lost three babies between my two sons. All were lost in early stages of pregnancy, "missed abortions." This means the fetus stopped developing and my body failed to eject it.

That's so me... like I can avoid the inevitable with sheer willpower.

Each loss was different and changed me. Sometimes I get the timeline and details confused. As the thought that I have more nameless could-have-been children to keep straight crosses my mind, I weep. It lets me know I still have hurt here needing healing.

When you experience a failed pregnancy you are inducted into a club. As you share, sisters come forward to share their stories too. You start to learn how many members are in this club, and it's startling.

REFLECTION

Have you been hesitant to share your story outside (or even within) your immediate circle? One of the greatest steps towards healing is stepping outside the walls of secrecy. Comfort is often found just outside of your comfort-zone. Connecting with others who have experienced miscarriage is important. You are not alone—far from it. One in four women experience the tragic pain of pregnancy loss through miscarriage. That's over one million miscarriages per year in the United States alone. Please don't feel like you have to stand strong and alone in secrecy. God's power shines brightest in our weakest moments. Just as much as you need someone to share with, they need you too. Healing is not a process to be done alone. And it's just that, a process. Just when you think you've got it together, a song, smell, date, or distant memory causes grief to flood in again. Sometimes the swells of sorrow are great and other times they roll over with a sense of peace. Regardless, the pain is present nonetheless. All of the contributors of this book will attest to the therapeutic healing that comes with sharing their stories. As you step out in faith to share *your* story, let hope and peace overcome any guilt or persevering pain.

ACTION

Share your story with someone today. Whether it be a close family member or friend, or even on social media, there is power in sharing. You're not alone.

If you share on social media, don't forget to use the hashtag #BrokenheartedHope.

DISCUSSION

1. What has held you back from sharing your story now or in the past? Are there feelings you've attempted to avoid such as pity, guilt, or pain?

2. Have you put up any "walls" based on these feelings? How have those walls affected the following relationships:
   - With your spouse?
   - With your friends/family?
   - With yourself?
   - With God?

3. Now that you've shared your story, reflect on it. How did it make you feel? Is it something you see yourself doing again?

Scripture

"But he said to me, 'My grace is sufficient for you, for my power is made perfect in weakness.' Therefore I will boast all the more gladly about my weaknesses, so that Christ's power may rest on me" (2 Corinthians 12:9).

CHAPTER 2: THESE FOUR WORDS
Thy Will be Done

---

*Looking back now, I can see God's
purpose through the pain, but it's hard to
see the rainbow in the midst of a storm.*

Whitney's Story

My husband and I got married with the intention of having
children right away. We are both teachers, and love kids. I
was in my mid-twenties and was ready to be a mother the day
I was born. However, it seemed the days of playing dress up
with my younger siblings and toting my baby dolls to every
mall, movie theater, and social gathering wasn't enough to
convince God that it was my time.

Looking back now, I can see God's purpose through the pain,
but it's hard to see the rainbow in the midst of a storm. I took
countless pills, numerous shots, tried twelve IUIs and
completed six rounds of IVF. Hope was all I had to cling to
in those dark days until the day I got my first positive.

17

The Dr. called with my blood work, as they did every month, and every single time I received a "no." For four years, all I heard was "I'm really sorry it didn't work. Is there anything I can do for you?" However, on this beautiful Friday after Thanksgiving, I heard my first "You're PREGNANT!"

I couldn't believe what I was hearing. My husband and I sobbed; we couldn't wait to share our news. We had always talked about cute ways to tell our families and had a Pinterest board full of ideas, but when you've waited so long, screaming "We are FINALLY going to have a baby!" at the top of your lungs doesn't seem too shabby.

Our families embraced us with tears as that precious, prayed-over grandchild, great-grandchild, niece/nephew was finally on his/her way. We went out for a special steak dinner that night with family and everyone doted over me. They opened my car door, gave me the last piece of bread, and worried I didn't need tea with caffeine because it might "harm the baby." All these years of waiting and it was everything I had dreamed of and more. This would be the first grandchild on my side, and the first one in 12 years on my husband's side.

We enjoyed the weekend on cloud nine and nothing could bring me down. Until Monday. I started bleeding at work and rushed to the doctor for more blood work. How could something change so drastically in three short days?

We grieved the loss of this precious baby, because even though it had only been a few days, I loved him/her like nothing I had ever loved before. Hope is what I clung to and hope is what God had given me. I had gotten pregnant one time, and I could get pregnant again according to my doctor.

It's one of those things where you are relieved to know you can get pregnant, but it still hurts nonetheless.

After seven more "no's," I finally got another "yes." This time we were cautiously optimistic. It wasn't pure joy with reckless abandonment like before, but rather "Will this one stick?"

We told our families and again everyone was excited, but nervous. Each day I could feel my stomach turn. Each doctor's visit I waited for more bad news, but it never came. Each checkup looked great and my blood work got stronger. It was to the point that the doctor and nurses were even thinking twins! I began to have serious pregnancy symptoms (including nausea), so I relaxed and enjoyed the journey because the doctor said there was no reason to worry this time.

I went to the beach with my family for a week. The day I got home, my husband and I excitedly anticipated hearing two heartbeats. On the way there we discussed names, in awe of how God decided to bless us after taking our other baby to Heaven.

As I lay on the table, my grin turned to tears. "I can't find a heartbeat. Your measurements look great and your blood work is great. We are going to give the baby the weekend to grow and we will try to listen again on Monday."

We were on our knees all weekend, begging God to let our baby grow. We cried out to Him for a miracle that would even amaze the doctor — something she would talk about for years to come.

We prayed, "Thy Will be done," and as the ultrasound showed no heartbeat on our next visit, His Will *was* done. Another one of our babies had gone to Heaven. Another reason why Heaven seemed so much sweeter. They scheduled my D&C for that Friday, and I dreaded it worse than twenty root canals. No one could prepare me to have a surgery to remove something that I so desperately wanted to keep. No one could have guarded my heart enough to prepare me to repeat to the nurses over and over again why I was there for the surgery and how far along I was. Nothing in this world can prepare for you for the pain you feel the minute they snap on your hospital bracelet. My miscarriage didn't feel real until they were wheeling me back. I guess I was in denial and thought that God could resurrect this baby the way He did Lazarus. Reality hit hard as they handed me my gown and made me put my clothes in a bag. With each tile my bed wheel rolled across, I could mentally see a trail of pieces of my broken heart fall behind me.

No one could prepare me to have a surgery to remove something that I so desperately wanted to keep.

Why did God allow me to have these precious gifts if He was only going to take them away? I could either run from God or to Him, and I'm so thankful He was there to catch me. He gave me the "no's" because my "yes" finally led to my miracle baby. We went through six years of infertility before I ever found my happily ever after. Not in my biological child, but an adopted child who is everything I prayed for and more. She has given me my joy back and God has used her to put those broken pieces of my heart back together. More importantly, He has given me a ministry through all that I have been through, and He has given my pain a purpose. I have sent cards, had countless encouraging phone calls, and prayed with and for other women who have experienced loss. My husband and I also led a small group for those experiencing infertility, miscarriage, and adoption loss. God has a way of allowing things to come full circle, and I wouldn't change one second of my story. If you are reading this, I'm praying for you and I can't wait to see your rainbow at the end of your storm.

I could either run from God or to Him and I'm so thankful He was there to catch me.

HEATHER'S STORY CONTINUED...

Winding roads on a dark night, a path I hadn't traveled before. Just me, my thoughts, and Christian songs playing on the radio. I was carrying the sting of hope lost and my mind raced as I attempted to anticipate the months ahead. But then my soul was stilled. As I heard the words, tears streamed down my face.

I felt an instant connection to the song. It wasn't until I was sharing my story with my boss that I understood why. A sister in Christ, due just a few weeks before me, sharing her heart and hope during her deepest sorrow through a melody.

I used to wonder how people could pray "Thy Will," knowing that pain might be a part of their purpose. I remember asking a friend who had lost a child if she was ever afraid to pray those words again. She and her husband had prayed for God's Will to be done from before conception to kneeling on the hospital floor after their son was miraculously born. Through their pain they cried out unselfishly with unswerving faith for God's Will and glory.

There's nothing like being completely out of control to show you who is in control of it all.

It wasn't until I had experienced the pain of loss myself that I truly understood how a person could pray those four words knowing the result could be pain. There's truly nothing like being completely out of control in a situation to show you who is in control of it all.

I realized that the deepest spiritual lessons are not learned by His letting us have our way in the end, but by His making us wait, bearing with us in love and patience until we are able to honestly pray what He taught His disciples to pray: Thy Will be done. — Elisabeth Elliot

---

REFLECTION

When heartbreak happens, it's so hard not to question why. Although you may be confused, you can be comforted in knowing that you don't have to lean on your own understanding to figure it out. With God we have the peace that surpasses all understanding living within us. There's no defeat in this world that can triumph over the eternal joy and glory that is the Lord. God has a plan and His thoughts and ways are higher than we could ever imagine. The Lord hears your cry and is working it all for your good. Cling to hope and have childlike faith knowing that God's pleasing and perfect Will is truly good. I know it doesn't feel good, but God sees what we cannot see. My pastor explained it simply once... Think about a child that has to get a shot or scrapes his or her knee. The parent knows that, although cleaning the wound or receiving the shot causes pain, ultimately it's for the child's good. Children trust their parents to do what's best. God is *our* Father. He is the beginning and the end. He goes before us and stands behind us. Scripture is filled with stories of people that endure pain in order to find their purpose. Faith is trusting God with your future. As you draw near to Him, your desires will align with His Will.

ACTION

As you read the scripture section below, take a deep breath after each verse and say, "I trust you, God." Then, say this simple prayer for God's Will to be done in your life:

> *Father God, You know the needs of my heart before the first tear falls from my face. Your Word is a lamp for my feet and a light on my path, for even the strongest heartaches. Though I don't always understand my hurt, I place my hope and confidence in the strength that is Your name. Lord, help me to see You in this time of heartache. Help me to avoid focusing on tribulation, but instead focusing on the fact that Your Word promises that You have overcome the world. Lord, I rejoice in Your sovereign Will because I know that it is perfect. Because you are at my right hand, I will not be shaken. Nothing is impossible for You. In Jesus' name I pray, Amen*

DISCUSSION

1. "There's nothing like being completely out of control to show you who is in control of it all." What does this quote mean to you? Are there areas of your life where you're holding on to control? How can you release these things to God today?

2. Have you been running *from* God or *to* Him? Why? How has this affected your acceptance of God's Will being carried out in your life?

3. Most people are familiar with saying, "Thy Will be done," as a part of the Lord's Prayer (Matthew 6:9-13). This was a model prayer Jesus used to teach his disciples how to pray. If God is all-powerful and "does whatever He pleases" (Psalm 115:3), then why do we need to pray for His Will to be done? Perhaps it's in order to help us align our hearts and actions with His purpose and plan for us. As you pray for God's Will to be done, you're surrendering your plans to His purpose. Looking back on your life, are there moments that you see God's Will playing into a greater purpose?

Scripture

"Trust in the Lord with all your heart; do not depend on your own understanding. Seek his Will in all you do, and he will show you which path to take" (Proverbs 3:5-6).

"I trust you, God."

"'My thoughts are nothing like your thoughts,' says the Lord. 'And my ways are far beyond anything you could imagine. For just as the heavens are higher than the earth, so my ways are higher than your ways
and my thoughts higher than your thoughts'" (Isaiah 55:8-9).

"I trust you, God."

"You intended to harm me, but God intended it all for good. He brought me to this position so I could save the lives of many people" (Genesis 50:20).

"I trust you, God."

"Then you will experience God's peace, which exceeds anything we can understand. His peace will guard your hearts and minds as you live in Christ Jesus" (Philippians 4:7).

"I trust you, God."

CHAPTER 3: PURPOSE IN THE PAIN
HIS PLAN IS PERFECT

---

*I don't have any choice but to praise Him
and trust Him, because without Him, there
is no purpose in my pain.*

RACHEL'S STORY

I will never forget the surprise of seeing those two lines. It was my very first natural pregnancy after years of infertility, an adoption, and a successful IVF.

I will never forget the immense joy, even if it meant I would have babies thirteen months apart. I will never forget the sound of that rapid heartbeat and the bright flashes on the screen at six weeks. I will never forget the way my heart dropped at the sight of blood at nine weeks. I will never forget the sight of a still baby on the ultrasound screen. I will never forget the face of my doctor telling me it was over. I will never forget the complete emptiness after waking up from a D&C. I will never forget the pain and grief that

27

followed for many months. I will never forget the community of believers coming alongside me. I will never forget the nearness of my God as He carried me through.

In Psalm 25:10 it says, "All the paths of the Lord are steadfast love and faithfulness." This truth from the Word of God has always been a favorite, but also sometimes a hard pill to swallow. Really God? *All* the paths? Even the painful ones?

It's hard when you go through a loss to not let the negative thoughts overcome you. Why would the Lord choose to give me such incredible joy, and then take it all away? I don't pretend to understand it. I don't pretend to like it.

A few weeks after my miscarriage as I read that verse, I knew that I still needed to praise God and trust His promise. I may not have felt like it, but in my praise I was choosing to surrender to the One who knows me intimately. The only One who can carry my pain.

Larry Crabb says in his book *Shattered Dreams*, "It's harder to discover our desire for God when things go well. We may think we have, but often all we've found is our desire to USE God, not to ENJOY Him. Shattered dreams are the truest blessings; they help us discover our true hope. But it can take a long, dark time to discover it."

The pain I feel and the storms I must go through in this life do not change who God is. He is Holy and He is good. That is the hope I have. I don't have any choice but to praise Him and trust Him because without Him there is no purpose in my pain.

The Lord alone determines our steps, and His plan is

sometimes one that we do not understand. For my husband and I, and perhaps for you too, it was a path of infertility and pregnancy loss. During my struggles I often cried out like the psalmist David, "How long must I take counsel in my soul and have sorrow in my heart all the day?" (Psalm 13:2). I have never felt sorrow or anguish like I felt month-after-month trying to get pregnant and again after a miscarriage.

However, God showed me more of His goodness, and some of His mysteriousness too. He truly worked wonders in my heart through infertility and loss. He led me to a place of joy and a time where I could sing to him with praise, even in the midst of incredible pain. I learned that sometimes God allows us to suffer, but it is in our suffering that He reveals His goodness.

It's okay to cry out to God with real emotion. There is something truly freeing when we confess it all to our Father. It's safe to say that we all want easy and pain-free lives, but if that were the case, we would never need God.

Suffering is a mystery and we see that in the Cross. It is the perfect picture of suffering and glory. God is so good and has dealt bountifully with us through His son. Through my pain (during infertility and after my loss), the Gospel came alive to me. I realized that even when times are hard, I'm able to sing and rejoice knowing that I have the greater hope of eternity.

In His faithfulness, the Lord has blessed us with four wonderful children. Our first came to us through the miracle of adoption. The second came to us through the miracle of In Vitro Fertilization. Our third came to us naturally and was the joy after mourning a miscarriage. Then, we had a surprise in our youngest. We have experienced almost every aspect of family planning you can go through. Honestly, it still overwhelms me. I feel so humbled when I think of how God decided to grow our family. I think Ephesians 3:20 sums it up pretty well: "Now to him, who is able to do immeasurably more than all we ask or imagine, according to his power that is at work within us."

Even if he had not blessed us with these four miracles, that verse would still ring true because the Lord also did immeasurably more work in my heart than I ever thought He could through my pain. He grew my heart for Him. He showed me that even though I long for control, I don't have it. He graciously grew my dependence on Him like never before. He was all I had (and He is all I have now)! I grew to understand that the story He was writing for my life was better than any I could write on my own. Even though we can't see the whole tapestry, He is weaving together beautiful threads for His glory in our lives. His love will never let you go. Run to Him and rest in knowing the work He is accomplishing through your pain.

Even though we can't see the whole tapestry, God is weaving together beautiful threads for His glory in our lives.

CHRISTA'S STORY

My first miscarriage happened when I was only seventeen; on Thanksgiving Day to be exact. Looking back, I know it was God's way of protecting me from a toxic relationship. I ran away from my family, not understanding that my parents saw something I didn't. I ended up being abused emotionally, physically and mentally by the so-called love of my life. I didn't listen to God or my family, and continued to endure the abuse. When I got pregnant again, the cruelty continued. Eventually, I returned home, experienced complications, and was put on bed rest. At 27 weeks I delivered a one-pound thirteen-ounce baby girl. What a miracle she was! A new beginning and beautiful rainbow after the storm.

After focusing on God, raising my daughter, and furthering my education, I met and married the true love of my life. By this time I was 28, and we knew we wanted to try getting pregnant right away. Months went by and nothing was happening. I remember feeling angry with God wondering why?

Almost a year later it finally happened. We were so excited and told family and close friends that we were expecting. I ended up losing the baby at around eight weeks. I saw the same doctor that delivered my baby girl just ten years prior. She confirmed that I was miscarrying, but didn't offer any reasoning as to why this would be happening again. It felt like there was no sympathy. I was shocked, confused, and again angry with God. Why God? Why are you allowing this to keep happening?

We moved on with our lives and decided to continue trying. Again, we saw those familiar pink lines. Although we were excited, I worried if I would be able to carry this baby to term. We felt led to change doctors and it was a blessing. The new doctor took time to listen to me. She confirmed our pregnancy and said everything looked good, but she wanted to do some additional testing.

We found out that I had what was called MTHFR, a gene mutation that can cause miscarriages, struggles getting pregnant, blood clots, heart issues, and much more depending on which mutation you have. She provided a plan and wanted to see me every other week to check the baby's progress. We were excited but still scared. When I went in for my nine-week checkup, the little one that we had already grown to love so much didn't have a heartbeat any longer. I immediately broke down crying in the doctor's office, so upset and angry at God once more.

The doctor prayed with me and promised she would do everything in her power to help us get a baby here healthy and full-term. We decided to let my body naturally take its course, but weeks later at my check-up I still needed medication to complete the "process." Even that didn't work and I ended up having a D&C. It felt like the pain would never end. I remember the day I went in for surgery sitting across from a lady who had just had her fourth child and was getting her tubes tied. I just cried and cried to God again, why God why?

When my doctor said we could start trying again, we prayed and prepared ourselves for the potential to lose another baby, but knew we had to try. I got pregnant right away and delivered a healthy baby boy. He is such a blessing and worth every negative pregnancy test, every miscarriage, and every cry to God. He was worth the wait! And now, as I write this, I am in the third trimester carrying another beautiful baby girl.

I tell this story because miscarriage is real. Infertility is real. Pregnancy doesn't always happen as beautifully as some might think. Sometimes it comes with struggles, tears, anger, and anxiety. We have to remember that God always has a plan and purpose for everything in our lives. Every season, He has perfectly planned out according to His purpose—not ours but His. It may not be an easy one, but it is His perfect plan.

Life's circumstances don't change God's character… He is forever Holy, faithful, and good.

REFLECTION

As women, many of us are natural planners. Life doesn't always happen how we'd like or might expect, but looking back, purpose can be found in the path – even when it includes pain. Faith comes from knowing God and trusting Him with the unknown. God loves you and wants you to experience the peace and abundant life He offers. The Bible says, "For God so loved the world that He gave His only begotten Son, that whoever believes in Him should not perish but have everlasting life" (John 3:16). He has a plan for you. Life's circumstances don't change God's character. Our outcomes don't determine His goodness. He is forever Holy, faithful, and good. But being at peace with God is not automatic. By nature, we are all separated from Him. The Bible says, "For all have sinned and fall short of the glory of God" (Romans 3:23). God is Holy, but we are human and don't measure up to His perfect standard. We are sinful, and "the wages of sin is death" (Romans 6:23). The good news is that God sent His Son to bridge the gap! When Jesus Christ died on the cross and rose from the grave, He paid the penalty for our sins. The Bible says, "'He Himself bore our sins' in His body on the cross, so that we might die to sins and live for righteousness; 'by His wounds you have been healed'" (1 Peter 2:24). If you're reading these testimonies and still wondering how, after such heartache, these women have hope for the future, the answer is surrender. This hope comes through salvation, God's gift of everlasting life. This gift is the greatest one you'll ever receive, and freely available to those who want it. You cross the bridge into God's family when you accept Christ's free gift of salvation. The Bible says,

"But as many as received Him, to them He gave the right to become children of God" (John 1:12). No matter what happens here on Earth, salvation provides hope for the future. The end is already written and (spoiler alert) God wins, but in your life it's up to you to give him the pen! If you've never invited God into your heart, or you feel like it's time to hand over your plans and heart again, pray this prayer of surrender:

God, I need you. I am a sinner. I humbly call out to you and release my timeline and plans. I ask for Your forgiveness and I turn away from my sins. I recognize the things I cannot control and praise You as the One who is in control of it all. Even now when it's hard to see through the pain, I have faith knowing there's purpose in Your plan. I believe Christ died on the cross and paid the debt for my sin. Thank you for sending Jesus to save me. I invite You to be my Lord and Savior, taking your rightful place as the number one priority in my life. Fill the emptiness in my heart with Your Holy Spirit and make me whole like only You can. Lord, help me to trust You and live my life for You. Help me to receive Your grace, mercy and peace as I praise You through the storm. I confess my sin and believe that it is through Christ alone, who bore that sin on the cross and died for me, that I am saved. Thank You for His resurrection and Your gift of salvation and eternal life. Thank You for the assurance that You will walk with me through the valleys and mountaintops — that I will never be alone. Thank You, God, for hearing this prayer and for providing this eternal hope. In Jesus' name I pray, Amen.

ACTION

Now that you've surrendered control to the One who is in control of it all, take some time to praise Him for this promise. After you read the scriptures below, whether you sit silently or sing like you're in the shower, praise Him for this gift of hope through song. Remind yourself that God's plan is perfect. Listen to your favorite worship music, or visit cravinggod.com/brokenheartedhope for a playlist that we have created just for you!

DISCUSSION

1. Are you a natural planner? What plans in your life have you made (or attempted to make) without consulting God first? What was the outcome?

2. Have you felt angry with God over the loss of your baby/babies? It's okay to cry out to God with emotion. Express your pain. Write out a prayer confessing your emotions, questions, and heartbreak to Jesus.

3. Now read Psalm 100:1-4. How can you show thankfulness and praise the Lord in the middle of this storm? What does this look like in your life?

Scripture

"In their hearts humans plan their course, but the LORD establishes their steps" (Proverbs 16:9).

"Many are the plans in a person's heart, but it is the LORD's purpose that prevails" (Proverbs 19:21).

"Now faith is confidence in what we hope for and assurance about what we do not see" (Hebrews 11:1).

"Every good and perfect gift is from above, coming down from the Father of the heavenly lights, who does not change like shifting shadows" (James 1:17).

"Your eyes saw my unformed body; all the days ordained for me were written in your book before one of them came to be" (Psalm 139:16).

"If you declare with your mouth, "Jesus is Lord," and believe in your heart that God raised him from the dead, you will be saved. For it is with your heart that you believe and are justified, and it is with your mouth that you profess your faith and are saved" (Romans 10:9-10).

"Shout for joy to the Lord, all the earth.
Worship the Lord with gladness;
come before him with joyful songs.
Know that the Lord is God.
It is he who made us, and we are his;
we are his people, the sheep of his pasture.
Enter his gates with thanksgiving

and his courts with praise;
give thanks to him and praise his name" (Psalm 100:1-4).

BROKENHEARTED HOPE

CHAPTER 4: FULLY KNOWN
OVERFLOWING PEACE

*God delivers on His timing if it is His
Will... He has you and I both in His
hands. He knows our hearts and desires.
He knows everything about us.*

ASHLEY'S STORY

We experienced loss while living abroad in Japan. I had just
come off birth control and we weren't really trying yet, but
had decided that we wanted to get pregnant around the time
we moved back to the United States. Everything happened so
fast.

I was six weeks along, so not far, but anyone who knows me
knows that I love babies and wholeheartedly believe I was
born to be a mother.

My first ultrasound was after the fact. As if it wasn't already
hard enough to accept, I had to see it too. Also add in the

fact that the doctor hardly spoke English, so we were trying to translate on our phones. It was horrific. I remember sitting on the sidewalk outside the office afterwards and calling my mom, hysterically crying. It was two o'clock in the morning her time, and she had no idea I was even pregnant to begin with. I hadn't even told my husband I was pregnant yet before it was already happening.

My husband is a very private, intellectual person. He's not as lovey-dovey as I am, but he was extraordinary in the months that followed. I wasn't quite sure how much he could handle on top of his already stressful work demands. The neediness I felt was so out of character from my usual independent self. I struggled immensely, questioning why God would give me this nurturing disposition from birth only to end in disappointment. I was just so heartbroken. I didn't know how to talk about it. Not wanting anyone's pity, I kept it to myself. I realized however, that's not God's design. Heartbreak should be shared and endured together, with all of the prayers and support you can get.

As I fell apart, my husband picked me up when I needed it the most. Our marriage was strengthened through the trial. I also had a very strong, close-knit group of women in my Bible study who were instrumental in guiding me back to God.

We decided to wait until Christmas to start trying again, mainly to give ourselves time to readjust to life back in America. We renovated our home and I got settled into working again. It didn't happen as quickly as before, but it happened nonetheless. As I write this, I am currently expecting a precious baby boy!

Of course I'm still nervous, and slightly overcautious, but God delivers on His timing if it is His Will. I've always been a planner, but I've learned over the years that my plans aren't always the best plans. He has you and I both in His hands. He knows our hearts and desires. He knows everything about us. God is my hope and always provides. That's what I know, trust, and love.

COURTNEY'S STORY

I still have days when it's hard, but I continue to trust that the same Creator and Author of life created my body and me just as perfectly as He created my Noah. He knows me and He knows you too.

Marriage and babies came early in my life. I got married the August after I graduated high school, and even though my mom pleaded with me during my entire engagement to wait to have kids, I was pregnant by October. It wasn't necessarily a planned pregnancy, but I celebrated this life because being a mother has always been the desire of my heart.

My first ultrasound didn't reveal the gender of my baby or the silhouette of its tiny body. What it did reveal was that I was in labor and there was nothing we could do to stop it. I was only 17 weeks along and labor had already progressed too far. My doctor gave me the option to go home and "pass it" or go to the hospital. I chose the hospital.

I was laying in the delivery room, the room where so many lives begin; knowing that this life was coming to an end. As the time grew closer I began to feel like the name we had picked out was not the name we were supposed to give this baby. Since we still didn't know the gender, we picked two new names from the Bible. Not long after that, it was time. My mom and mother-in-law sat on a small sofa in the corner. My husband held my right hand and a nurse held my left.

My favorite worship song played on repeat. Two pushes and he was out. Immediately, they rushed him out of the room to examine him. They needed to determine if the problem was with his body or mine. We all cried. The nurse brought him back in and said that he was perfect. She placed him in my arms and immediately Psalm 139 came to mind: "For you created my inmost being; you knit me together in my mother's womb. I praise you because I am fearfully and wonderfully made; your works are wonderful, I know that full well" (v. 13-14). I grew up hearing this passage, but in that moment, I understood what it truly meant.

His eyes and nose were shaped like my husband's and his second toe was longer than his first. His translucent skin revealed the tiny veins that flowed through his body. He had tiny fingernails and toenails. Not only was my sweet Noah perfectly knit together by our Creator, but he was known by Him.

After everyone left and it was finally quiet, my husband and I were left to process the events of the last 24 hours. Out of curiosity my husband looked up the meaning of the name Noah. When the words "rest and comfort" came up, we began to cry. I thought back to the urgency I had hours before to change the names. We knew from the very beginning that God was holding us close, but this was such a gift.

The next few days were some of my hardest. A visit to a funeral home, buying clothes that hid my empty belly, wearing cabbage leafs and bandages to dry up my milk, and hiding the onesies, blankets, and the "My 1st Christmas" ornament we had already bought. As hard as those days were, they were also filled with peace and an outpouring of love. We were able to share with others the beauty and perfection that grew inside of me. We told people about the gift that his name was, about the gift that his life was. We received a peace from the Almighty that overflowed from us, allowing us to provide comfort to our family. There was truly beauty in the ashes.

I was later diagnosed with an incompetent cervix. It would take years for me to accept the fact that my body had failed and would continue to do so. My body might never be strong enough to carry a baby to full term on its own. I had to trust that God gave me the desire to be a mother when I was just a child, and He would be faithful. Almost nine years have passed and I now have three beautiful children that know of their older brother who is waiting for us in Heaven! I still have days when it's hard, but I continue to trust that the same Creator and Author of life created my body and me just as perfectly as He created my Noah. He knows me and He knows you too. I pray that you find comfort in that today.

REFLECTION

God designed our bodies and our babies too. He makes no mistakes and we are made perfectly in His image (Genesis 1:27). God knows us completely. There are things in this life we will never know, but one day we will know completely, just as we are fully known. Not only do our lives have purpose, but our babies' lives have purpose too. Sometimes it's the littlest feet that make the biggest footprints on the heart. When the burden is too heavy to bear, find rest, comfort, and peace in the Lord. Share your heart and hope with others. The gift you've received isn't something to keep to yourself! Let God's love overflow. There's no greater testimony than the light of hope and peace despite the darkness. If you haven't already started a journal to answer discussion questions and record your story, meaningful scripture, and prayers, start today. It's amazing to look back in life at the ways God is faithful. As you dive deeper into God's Word and meet Him daily in thankfulness, praise, and prayer, you'll grow intimately in your relationship with Him.

ACTION

In addition to the scriptures below, read Isaiah 61:1-3 and reflect on the verses. Let God's peace wash over you as you study His Word.

DISCUSSION

1. As women, so much focus is placed on our bodies. We feel constant pressure to be perfect. Read Psalm 139:13-14. Not only did God knit your baby perfectly in your womb, He made you perfect too! What are ways that you can find comfort in knowing God created you perfectly and knows you fully?

2. Do you feel "weary and burdened?" In Matthew 11:28-30, we're instructed to take Jesus' yoke upon us. A yoke is a wooden crosspiece that is fastened to the neck of two animals and attached to the cart or plow they pull. They are attached and bear the burden of the weight together. Neither of them carries the full load. What are some practical ways in your life that you can "attach" to Jesus and experience rest?

Scripture

"Now we see things imperfectly, like puzzling reflections in a mirror, but then we will see everything with perfect clarity. All that I know now is partial and incomplete, but then I will know everything completely, just as God now knows me completely" (1 Corinthians 13:12).

"Before I formed you in the womb I knew you, before you were born I set you apart; I appointed you as a prophet to the nations." (Jeremiah 1:5).

"Come to me, all you who are weary and burdened, and I will give you rest. Take my yoke upon you and learn from me, for I am gentle and humble in heart, and you will find rest for your souls. For my yoke is easy and my burden is light." (Matthew 11:28-30).

"And I declared that the dead, who had already died, are happier than the living, who are still alive. But better than both is the one who has never been born, who has not seen the evil that is done under the sun" (Ecclesiastes 4:2-3).

"So that Christ may dwell in your hearts through faith. And I pray that you, being rooted and established in love, may have power, together with all the Lord's holy people, to grasp how wide and long and high and deep is the love of Christ" (Ephesians 3:17-18).

CHAPTER 5: FREE TO GRIEVE
KNOW WHAT YOU NEED

Jesus wanted me to need Him and only Him all along. He wanted to wrap His arms around me and give me all-consuming peace. When I put my trust in Him and thanked Him for what He had given me, He supplied my greatest need.

JESSICA'S STORY

I found out I was pregnant with our second baby in October of 2013. It was not expected, but it was welcomed. We were excited! We had fertility issues with our first, so it was refreshing to learn that we could become pregnant without fertility assistance. I went to the doctor to get my HCG levels checked to make sure the pregnancy was viable. The first blood results came back and confirmed my pregnancy. That instilled the hope; hope that this baby was happy, healthy, and growing. I never for a second worried about this baby. I had no reason to worry! I had been pregnant before and everything was fine.

At the time, my husband was out of town in Alabama. We lived in Texas, but knew we would be moving for his job within the year. He asked that I come visit him to see if I could envision this place as a temporary home for our family. I left that weekend to see him. I had already told him over the phone about our exciting news. My husband was in medical school, so he had a substantial understanding about early pregnancy and the risks that accompany it, especially when you have had previous fertility issues. In turn, he was not as giddy and excited as I was when I met him at the airport. At first it hurt my feelings, but in hindsight I know he was being the grounded man that God designed him to be.

I knew within the next day or so that I would be receiving my second HCG blood results, but honestly, I didn't think about it. I felt pregnant, so no need to worry. Then they called. She said in a sterile, almost robotic voice that my HCG levels had dropped. She explained that meant the pregnancy was not viable, and that I would miscarry within the next day or so. My world stopped; I felt like someone knocked the breath out of me. My husband looked at me and immediately knew what was said on the other end of the phone. He hugged me and told me he was so sorry. We didn't know what to do. How long would it take? When would I start bleeding? How did this happen? Why me? Why?

I started spotting an hour later. We went up to the hotel room where for the next two hours I contracted and miscarried my baby into a white hotel toilet. This mortified me. I felt so alone. I had hope in this pregnancy. It had already pulled me in, and I was invested. My husband, on the other hand, hadn't connected with the pregnancy the way that I had. I was angry. I needed him to scoop me up and hold me for hours. I needed him to get my baby out of the toilet and put it in the ground.

The next day I decided to move on. I didn't grieve anymore. I knew I had a little girl to get back to, so I flew away from Alabama and home to my child.

Fast-forward to May of 2016 when I found out I was pregnant again. This time we did have fertility assistance. Of course I was excited, but after the initial excitement wore off, I completely froze. For the first twelve weeks I didn't leave my couch. I was so afraid that my baby would leave my body before she was supposed to. After the first trimester, I started to be more hopeful, but I was still anxious. I was constantly Googling and finding out horrible things that could be wrong with my baby.

In hindsight, I had never dealt with the trauma of my miscarriage, and Satan used that against me to turn my anxiety into all-consuming fear. I prayed and begged God for peace. At first I didn't understand. Why didn't God make my husband get up and hold me during the miscarriage? Why would He not give me peace during this pregnancy? These questions haunted me until one night at church when I felt the Holy Spirit speaking the word "need" over me.

That night, as we sang one of my favorite songs about needing Jesus every moment, it suddenly hit me. I needed to grieve. I also needed to stop stressing over the things outside of my control. All I needed was Jesus. That night I raised my hands and thanked God for my healthy babies and for my husband. Jesus wanted me to need Him, and only Him, all along. He wanted to wrap His arms around me and give me all-consuming peace. When I put my trust in Him, stopped living in fear, and thanked Him for what He had given me, He supplied my greatest need. The peace was greater than I could have imagined and so much better than anything I ever could have thought I might have needed.

Brooke's Story

In the spring of 2010, my life was in shambles. I was in a marriage that felt completely hopeless, but in the middle of the chaos, the Lord sent me a tiny miracle. I will never forget the day I realized I was a few days late. I thought to myself that there was no way I was pregnant. I hadn't missed any pills, so my cycle must have been a little off from all the stress. When I saw that positive pregnancy test, a wave of emotions swept over me. I sat in my bathroom staring at those double pink lines. I knew that precious baby and I (and my then-four-year-old son) were going to be fine regardless of the outcome of the situation. That precious sign of life gave me a joy I hadn't felt in years.

We shared the news with family and friends and two weeks later, when I went in for my first prenatal appointment, all appeared to be well. They confirmed my pregnancy and we went through the routine process for getting everything in place for my prenatal care. I had already begun to experience the normal morning sickness and fatigue just as I had with my first pregnancy. Everything seemed to be on track and, while a lot of things around me were crumbling, I clung to my faith and this hope.

I went in for my first ultrasound and after a few moments passed, I heard the ultrasound tech say, "Let me get the doctor in here." That statement was never said to me when I was pregnant with my first. All I knew was that the sweet little heartbeat that I was supposed to be hearing wasn't filling the room. My heart sank and I knew immediately that something wasn't right. My mind began to race. I felt sick and anxious all over. I had only known I was pregnant for just shy of a month, but in that month this baby had my heart.

It felt like an eternity before the doctor joined us in that dark room; a room that had suddenly turned from joyous anticipation to heartbreak and fear. My doctor then told me that the baby had simply stopped growing. My eight-week-old baby was measuring only five weeks. He called the miscarriage a blighted ovum. There might have been an empty sac, but I had an even emptier hole in my heart. I had never heard that term before, but honestly all I heard was that I wasn't getting my baby in seven months like I had hoped.

Tears began to soak my face and the front of my gown. I felt like someone had ripped my heart out. I could feel myself slowly slipping into a deep depression, and I had not even left the ultrasound room. I begged God to be my strength, and to physically help me get out of that doctor's office and into my car.

I went home that afternoon and took a few white pills and within hours the most terrible cramps and bleeding started. I sat on my bathroom floor and wept, doubled over in pain for what felt like forever. It couldn't be over soon enough, but unfortunately the symptoms lasted for days.

Soon after, my body started to go back to normal, but everything in my personal life turned upside down. Because of all that I was dealing with, I found myself sweeping the loss aside. My emotions couldn't handle much more, so I put that devastating event on a shelf in the back of my mind where I could unpack it at a later date.

Fast-forward four years. I had remarried, celebrated our one-year wedding anniversary, and closed on our first home. I felt like the Lord had truly started to make beauty from the ashes. In December 2014, I knew my cycle was late. My husband and I were actively trying to get pregnant, and I was counting the days until I could take a test. I will never forget being in our hall bathroom and staring at a double pink line. I hadn't seen those lines since the spring of 2010! I was thrilled, but naturally anxious and full of worry. I couldn't wait for time to pass so I could hear my baby's heartbeat; a heartbeat that I never heard with my last.

Our precious baby boy was born, and after a short stay in the NICU, we brought him home. To say that I was grateful for my rainbow baby was an understatement. Soon after getting home, however, postpartum started creeping in. I remember sitting in my lounge chair pumping milk when those familiar waves of depression washed over me.

It was strange in that, as I sat there and stared at my beautiful baby boy sleeping right next to me, all I could think about was my angel baby that I lost. It was then that I fully realized I hadn't properly grieved the loss. My emotions turned from sadness to guilt for feeling this way during a time I should be happy and thankful. I couldn't escape it and the pain was more than I could handle on my own.

I wanted my angel baby to know that I loved it so very much, missed it more than I could stand, and I wanted it to know that I was sorry for not dealing with all of this sooner. I didn't want it to think that it had been replaced by its baby brother or forgotten. I asked the Lord to convey these things to my baby in Heaven. I prayed for the Lord to guide me through these feelings, and to help me properly deal with my emotions in order to achieve peace and move forward.

Eventually, I realized that Satan was using this as a stumbling block to fill my mind with doubt, negativity, depression, worthlessness, and so many other emotions to distract me from my walk with the Lord and from being the mother my other children needed. He was using this loss to tear me down and distract me from the good things the Lord had brought into my life. Soon after this, I felt a slow healing begin. I told God that I would leave it at the foot of the cross. I knew that I would still have times of hurt and struggle, but I couldn't allow it to continue to bring me down.

That Christmas, I was unpacking ornaments and came across a tiny pair of angel wings I had purchased a few years back in memory of my baby. As I hung them on our tree, not too far from the boys' first Christmas ornaments, I felt a mixture of sadness and peace all at once. I whispered out loud to my precious baby in Heaven, "Mommy loves and misses you and I will see you again one day." It was then that I knew the Lord had delivered me from a place of grief, depression, and sadness and set my feet upon a solid rock.

REFLECTION

When you experience loss of any kind, it's important to allow yourself to grieve. We try to be so strong, but it's important to acknowledge grief and know what you need. Out of sight is not out of mind. Suppressed grief gives the enemy a stronghold for things like distraction, depression, and debilitating fear. The greatest need in grief is to acknowledge it, and give it to God. Allow yourself to feel the pain. Have a good cry if you need it. It's okay to cry. Grief is also relative. Many times women experience feelings of guilt for their grief. I've heard women say, "but I wasn't very far along," or "I know others experience greater loss." Every loss is a loss, and it's relative to your life. You felt the hope of what once was, and now that it's gone, it's a loss to be mourned. But with Jesus, grief can turn from sadness to hope through eternal life. You'll trade your sackcloth (mourning garment) for joy and your faithfulness will bring glory to God. We can rejoice here on Earth knowing that we will one day see our babies again in Heaven!

ACTION

Pray and ask God to search your heart and reveal any untouched grief. Ask God for protection against the enemy, and to turn your grief to peace. Know that your greatest need is Jesus. Know that Jesus understands, as He too experienced grief. Read John 11:1-37. Jesus went to Bethany to bring his friend back to life. When He approached the tomb, although He knew Lazarus would wake, He was troubled and deeply moved by the grief of those around Him. But then something beautiful happened... Jesus called Lazarus from darkness into the light!

Father God, help me to remember that You are big enough to hear all of my cries, all of my hurts, and all of my emotions. Lord, I know that when I grieve, You grieve with me, but You also leave me with a hope knowing that you bind the wounds of my broken heart. Your Word reminds me that You do not give us a spirit of fear, but of love, strength, and sound mind. Lord, help me to grieve in love for the loss of this precious baby. Though my weeping may endure for the night, I know my joy comes in the morning. Lord, search my heart and show me what I may have hidden away in fear that needs to be placed at Your feet. Father God, thank you for hearing my prayers...the ones that may only come out as a sob, but You know every grief that is in my heart. You care for me, and with that I am blessed. In Jesus' name I pray, Amen.

DISCUSSION

1. Have you grieved over your loss, or do you find yourself "pushing it aside" in order to continue on with your life? As mentioned above, "Suppressed grief gives the enemy a stronghold for things like distraction, depression, and debilitating fear." How have you seen this play out in your life? What are some ways the enemy is using this against you? What do you think are ways these strongholds can be destroyed?

2. As you read John 11:1-37, did you find comfort in the fact that Jesus Himself experienced grief? How does this change the way that you view grieving your loss?

Scripture
"When he heard this, Jesus said, "This sickness will not end in death. No, it is for God's glory so that God's Son may be glorified through it" (John 11:4).

"Blessed are those who mourn, for they will be comforted" (Matthew 5:4).

"For his anger lasts only a moment, but his favor lasts a lifetime; weeping may stay for the night, but rejoicing comes in the morning" (Psalm 30:5).

"You turned my wailing into dancing; you removed my sackcloth and clothed me with joy, that my heart may sing your praises and not be silent. Lord my God, I will praise you forever" (Psalm 30:11-12).

CHAPTER 6: STRENGTH TO YOUR STEPS
TURN TO HIM

God takes heartbreak and uses it for His purpose. That's where I find my strength to overcome and the courage to share our Hope in Christ.

JONATHAN'S STORY

In many ways, Ashleigh is a part of our everyday lives. When her siblings speak of her they do so fondly, as if talking about a friend. My wife and I talk about all the things she might have done, who she might have become, and what she might have accomplished. I find myself thinking about whom she might have favored. Brown eyes? Blue eyes? Dark hair? Light hair? Short? Tall? Time has allowed this process to become easier, and I look forward to the day that I get to meet her.

May 16, 2006, began as any other day. My wife and I met at the doctor's office for a 12-week checkup, as we were expecting our second child. At that time we had been married for three years, and had an 18-month-old daughter. We had recently shared the news with family and close friends. This pregnancy was even more exciting because we had trouble conceiving, and needed help with our first child. This newest addition was coming as a surprise with no assistance from doctors. We felt blessed by God in all areas of our life and now, He was allowing our family to grow once again.

While in the exam room, the nurse was having trouble locating the heartbeat. She attributed it to still being early in the pregnancy. The office wasn't busy that morning, so she took us to the ultrasound room. In the few lingering minutes of silence, I became aware of what was possibly going on. The once active little girl on the screen lay completely still as if she was asleep.

The nurse excused herself momentarily, as she needed to compose herself and get the attention of our doctor. He entered the room as my wife and I both tried to grasp what was happening. He took control of the ultrasound and uttered the words, "I'm so sorry." We could not have asked for a better doctor and staff during this time. As the doctor tried his best to explain how common this was, I attempted to understand. As an analytical person, I needed answers. I wanted a concrete explanation. What went wrong? What did we do wrong? Unfortunately, as I learned over the next few minutes, hours, and days, sometimes there are no answers to be found.

Afterwards, I was very hard on myself. Naturally, as the head of our household, when I found out we were expecting again my thoughts were a mixture of excitement, fear, and anxiety about a growing family. Could we "afford" a second child so soon? Candidly, prior to losing Ashleigh, I felt myself at times wishing we weren't expecting. This is a thought that still haunts me to this day. The guilt I have felt at times has been overwhelming. There was a time when that guilt turned to anger towards God. I was angry that somehow it was Him who took Ashleigh away. Did he do it because of my thoughts? Was it something else? What made it even more difficult is that I had only recently given my life to Christ. I had grown up in church and knew the Gospel, but I did not have a personal relationship with Jesus. After losing Ashleigh I struggled with my faith.

Work was where I found my escape. I kept myself busy and didn't talk about it. Even today, it is hard at times to speak with anyone openly about Ashleigh. But I have learned that God has used this as a way for both my wife and I to reach out to others. Sharing our story has helped with the healing process.

Additional healing came from a very unexpected place. Through the eyes and words of a child, God let us know everything was okay and was going to be okay.

All three of our children had the opportunity to attend a community Bible study with their grandmother. They had classes that were designed to introduce Bible stories through arts and crafts and songs. Twice a year the different age groups would put on a concert of sorts and sing for their parents. It was always fun to watch, especially the younger ones, as you never knew what they might do!

Following one of these concerts, our daughter made reference to Ashleigh. We had spoken about her on occasion, and she seemed to understand even at such a young age that she had a sister in Heaven. But it was what she said next, that to this day makes me stop in my tracks.

She said, "I saw Ashleigh today. She came to watch me sing and had an angel with her. It was very bright and she sat up by the window in the back of the room." I was stunned in silence and found myself not wanting to believe because I didn't understand. It goes against everything I thought I knew or understood. In a strange way, I felt a little bit of jealousy that she got to see her. I realized that God was using this as an opportunity to remind us that Ashleigh was real, and she was with Him, safe and sound.

Fast-forward a couple of years, and a similar situation occurred with our son, in the same place while also singing. He, too, told us about seeing Ashleigh and that she had come to hear him sing. Many years have passed since our children saw their sister in that window while singing praise songs to God, but they still speak of her as if she has been a part of their lives here on Earth.

We take time to specifically celebrate her life twice a year. My wife and I privately celebrate the memory of the day we lost her, and as a family we celebrate what would have been her birthday. We typically purchase a balloon, attach a note to Ashleigh, and watch it fly up to her as we let it go. The kids really enjoy doing this, and I have to say that I do as well.

---

*Husbands can struggle to show or share
their emotion following a miscarriage, and I*

think it has more to do with trying to be a
strong, silent protector for their wife.

As the husband and father in this situation, I found myself focusing my attention on my wife. I had to be her comforter and protector, and felt like a voice of reason. While physically everything was happening to her, both of us were suffering mentally and spiritually. Husbands can struggle to show or share their emotion following a miscarriage, and I think it has more to do with trying to be a strong, silent protector for their wife. However, it is of extreme importance to seek God and surround yourself with Christian brothers who are not only there for you, but also offer counsel and a listening ear. It is not a quick process to get to a place of acceptance knowing God's plan is perfect. It is with certainty that we will face heartbreak here on Earth, but God takes heartbreak and uses it for His purpose. That is where I find my strength to overcome and the courage to share our hope in Christ.

DeLisa's Story

My story of loss is a story I have now lived with for 22 years. I was twenty-eight years old, married, and the mother of a beautiful little girl who was 15 months old and stepmother to a 14-year-old daughter and 16-year-old son. My husband and I found out we were pregnant with a son, due February 19, 1995.

This pregnancy was a little more difficult than my first, but still fairly uneventful. Five days before my due date, I had contractions that were strong enough to send me to the hospital. The doctor examined me, performed an ultrasound, and decided the contractions were mild and not worthy of a hospital stay, so I was sent home.

On my due date I got out of bed and ran to the restroom. The contractions I had felt before had started again, but became stronger. My husband and I jumped into the car and headed towards the hospital. Within a mile of the hospital, my contractions were so strong and so close together, I was terrified I wouldn't make it there. As the nurse took me into the room, they discovered bleeding and seemed concerned. She put belts around my abdomen (remember this is 1995) to listen to my son's heartbeat. She made a strange face and said, "Hmm, I'm going to get the ultrasound machine. I'm just not hearing the heartbeat the way I'd like." I didn't get worried at the time because, frankly, I thought nothing bad could ever happen to me. I followed all the rules, didn't smoke or drink, took care of myself, etc. There just couldn't be anything truly wrong.

I remember the doctor-on-call coming in with a somber look on his face and not saying much. He hooked up the ultrasound machine, ran the wand across my belly, and turned and looked at me. He quietly said, "I'm very sorry, his heart isn't beating."

My husband collapsed to the floor, and I felt my body go numb. I could no longer feel contractions or pain, just numbness. I remember looking at him and saying, "What do you mean? Is he gone?"

He just said, "Yes, I'm so sorry." My immediate thoughts were so jumbled. I couldn't process what I was hearing. How could this happen? I prayed that this was a mistake, a bad dream, anything. I tried to make deals with God to "fix" this. Unfortunately, I had to face a reality I wasn't ready to accept.

I gave birth to my son several hours later. The silence was deafening. I kept waiting to hear his cries, but only heard silence. The cause of death…cord accident. I didn't even know such a thing existed. The funeral was a complete blur. I remember the songs that played, and what seemed like hundreds of people hugging me. I remember my husband reading a poem he'd written.

In the weeks after the funeral, I was angry with God. I cried every time I heard a baby cry. How could this have happened? What did I do to deserve this? What did I do to CAUSE it? The loss took its toll on my marriage, but I made the conscious decision not to let it take a toll on my faith. I was raised in Christian schools as a child and knew that my only saving grace would be for me to turn back to the scriptures I remembered.

This is still painful for me to talk about to this day. Even though I'm remarried and have three daughters, I still wonder what raising James Edward would have been like. Would he look like me? Would he be athletic like his dad? Would he pester his sisters? What would he have become?

JANIE'S STORY

All Dressed in pink a lovely sight
For your family you'll be a true delight
Baby dolls and stuffed animals will surround

. Around your little fingers Mom and Dad will be wound
Welcome to this world, Malley Jane
And by the way, you have a lovely, unusual name
- Edna Rouse (2/16/2013)

This was a poem given to us by a sweet, precious older lady in our church for our first baby shower. She was true in what she wrote. Malley Jane was a name, that four years later, people would still remember.

On July 9, 2012, my 27th birthday, I found out that I was pregnant with our firstborn child, Malley Jane. This was a time for my husband and I to rejoice and look forward to the new beginnings that God had so graciously blessed us with. We were excited for the restoration of our lives, coming from the brokenness and mistakes of our past.

I had a very healthy pregnancy. At every ultrasound Malley Jane showed her personality; from hiccupping and moving in different ways, to showing us her pouty face during the 3D ultrasound! She did already have us wrapped around her finger. She had a family that loved her, prayed for her, and could not wait for her to arrive. I wrote down every detail about each doctor visit, feeling the kicks during the Christmas Cantata, having the grandmothers slow down on buying EVERYTHING in stores, and of course, Daddy singing and reading the Bible to her every night. This was our time — our time to have our little family.

On March 2nd, regardless of our perfect preparation, our whole world drastically changed within a few short hours. That morning, I was sitting in our recliner writing in her memory book, so thankful for what God was about to give us. It was finally the day to see my precious daughter!

After cooking breakfast with my mom, I felt a trickle down my leg. It was time! My husband called our doctor, and we immediately went to the hospital. Things got a little hectic. I remember it so clearly, but some parts I want to forget. The perfect world that I had planned would soon come crashing down.

I was rushed in to have an emergency C-section, only to have our child born without time to take her first breath. Malley Jane went nine minutes without oxygen. This was the beginning of God's journey and our obedience.

I knew as a follower of Christ, I had to make a decision in my mind. As I heard words like funeral and death, tears flowed as I tried so desperately to hear the faintest cry. Nothing. I had to decide right then and there… Let this world take over me and my mind, or allow God to use this situation for His glory.

I prayed aloud in the room. I cried out for family to pray. I stared into my husband's eyes and just kept saying she is going to be all right… she is. Only to see in the neonatal surgeon's eye that that was not what was happening.

Malley Jane was born at 7:38 weighing 6lbs 15oz and 20 inches long. She lived three glorious weeks in the NICU in Jackson, Mississippi, fighting for her life. In those weeks she impacted more souls on this earth than I ever could in this lifetime. You see, we made a decision to give Malley to God, and God so graciously took our story and impacted over 46,000 people across the world through social media. People were praying for her day and night. Twenty-seven people (that we know of) came to know the Lord. To this very day she still impacts so many.

Instead of drowning in sorrow and questioning why, God provided a reason to pray. I could probably write a book about grief, and the journey that God set before us, because the story doesn't end there. Ahead of us was still the normal anger, depression, and questions you ask that only God can heal.

God is still writing that chapter of our lives. I just know that I serve a mighty God whom I find my comfort. He is the healer of all our stripes. He directs our paths, and every step that seems so impossible to take, He takes for us.

He is the healer of all our stripes. He directs our paths, and every step that seems so impossible to take, He takes for us.

March 23, 2013, we buried our Malley Jane, but she forever lives in us and through us. You see, God continues to restore our souls through every part of life. Not only have I buried a child, but I have also experienced two miscarriages since. Every loss was different and broke my heart, but every time, God was there to pick me up. Every child is received into the arms of God. What a glorious day it will be when I can rejoice with my babies. For now, we live this life the best we know how. Every part of life I go through, and share with others, only helps with the healing.

Since Malley, we had another daughter, and now are expecting a baby boy. The one thing I want you to think of as you read just a glimpse of our lives, is that as trials and tribulations come your way.... don't run from Him... run to Him. Run into His arms and never let go.

As trials and tribulations come your way, don't run from Him, run to Him. Run into God's arms and never let go.

REFLECTION

In the midst of tragedy, we have a choice. It's natural to ask questions and wonder why. To dream about what once was and could have been. It's so very important, instead of running away from God, to turn to Him. Surround yourself with other believers that will listen and lift you up. Healing is a process that takes time — a process that may never be fully complete this side of Heaven. Trials on Earth are certain, but God is the one thing that is sure. When there are days you have no strength to your steps, let God carry you through. Let this purpose provide courage to share your hope in Christ. As each of these testimonies has attested, there is healing power in sharing your story and hope.

ACTION

How do you grow your relationship with your spouse, family, or friends? You SPEND TIME with them. A growing relationship with God comes when you experience Him often. Turn to God's Word daily for encouragement. If you don't have a scheduled time or everyday plan to meet with God, make one today. Your quiet time can be as simple as reading scripture and reflecting in your journal. You can also spend time with God through praise and worship or prayer. Better yet, how about a balance of all of all three? Don't get overwhelmed. It's not about *how much* you do… It's about meeting with God right where you are. Turn to Him and let His strength guide your steps.

DISCUSSION

1. Have you turned to other things in order to "escape" the reality of your loss? How has this affected your life and walk with Christ?

2. Read Jeremiah 29:12-14. Seek God's face and not His hand. What does this mean? You can tell a lot about a person by looking at their face. Are they happy, sad, angry, etc.? The face of a person is like an open window that allows us to see inside their soul—their thoughts, their pain, their joy and their heart. To seek God's face is to enter into God's heart. To seek God's hand, on the other hand, is more focused on *us* and *our desires* rather than His. It's a "what can you do for me" mentality. But when you seek God with ALL of your heart, your heart will align with His. Regardless of what's going on around you, you will have unfathomable freedom and peace. Are you seeking God's hand or face?

Scripture

"Draw near to God and He will draw near to you" (James 4:8).

"But He *was* wounded for our transgressions, He was bruised for our iniquities; the chastisement for our peace *was* upon Him, and by His stripes we are healed" (Isaiah 53:5).

"The Lord is close to the brokenhearted and saves those who are crushed in spirit" (Psalm 34:18).

"Then you will call upon Me and go and pray to Me, and I will listen to you. And you will seek Me and find Me, when you search for Me with all your heart. I will be found by you, says the LORD, and I will bring you back from your captivity; I will gather you from all the nations and from all the places where I have driven you, says the Lord, and I will bring you to the place from which I cause you to be carried away captive" (Jeremiah 29: 12-14).

"Look to the Lord and his strength; seek his face always" (Psalm 105:4).

"My soul clings to the dust;
Revive me according to Your word.
I have declared my ways, and You answered me;
Teach me Your statutes.
Make me understand the way of Your precepts;
So shall I meditate on Your wonderful works.
My soul melts from heaviness;

Strengthen me according to Your word"
(Psalm 119:25-28).

"Your word is a lamp for my feet, a light on my path" (Psalm 119:105).

"He gives strength to the weary and increases the power of the weak" (Isaiah 40:29).

CHAPTER 7: GOD IS FAITHFUL
BEAUTIFUL BLESSINGS

I am thankful God allowed me to miscarry because I can now share with other women that He is the only one who can ever fill that hole in your heart from losing a child.

BROOKE'S STORY

I was eighteen when I took a pregnancy test on a hot August day, and found out I was pregnant for the first time. I was scared, angry, upset, embarrassed, and ashamed, but there was a tiny part of me that was also a little excited. I've always loved children, and I've always dreamed of the day I would have my very own. However, I never dreamed that day would be when I was only eighteen.

My boyfriend and I got married, bought a house, and started building our new life as a family. I got an amazing job at the corporate office of a local chain restaurant and we were living the so-called "American Dream," even if we were young. We made our first doctor's appointment and even got to see our baby, Peyton, in an ultrasound. We were able to listen to Peyton's heartbeat and take home several pictures. I was 10 weeks pregnant, and at my next appointment we would get to sneak a peek and see if Peyton was a girl or boy!

One Thursday night in late October, I went to the bathroom and realized something wasn't right. I called my mom, who is a nurse, and she met me at the ER. They did an ultrasound and we could see Peyton's face, arms, and legs, but there was one difference... Peyton was not wiggling like in the ultrasound before. The doctor confirmed what I feared. I had lost my baby.

The next few days were a complete blur. I had surgery and my doctor offered to call me when he got the pathology results to let me know if Peyton was a boy or a girl. I was numb. I didn't want to know anything. I didn't want to do anything. I just wanted this to all be over and to be able to move forward with my new family. I was in complete shock and denial.

Over the next several weeks, part of me was relieved because it was never in my plan to have a baby so young. Then came the guilt I felt from feeling relieved in the first place. There was also another part of me that had grown accustomed to the thought of being a young mother who desperately wanted a baby.

Throughout this whole process, I was so mad at God. I didn't understand why He would ever allow this to happen to me! I went to church every time the doors were open. I had always been involved and I asked Him into my heart when I was seven! I didn't drink, do drugs, or smoke. I didn't skip school or stay out past curfew. The problem with my thoughts, and my relationship with Jesus at that time, was that it was based on me and what I had done, instead of being focused on Him. I was completely lost and I didn't even realize it.

Fast-forward six years, and I now have one daughter, got divorced from my first husband, and married an amazing godly man. My life was completely different and everything I ever dreamed of and more. I was truly living out the dreams I had of who and what my family would consist of from when I was a little girl.

My husband and I had been married for a little over a year when we decided to start trying to have a baby. We started trying in January and found out in May that we were expecting. We were elated! We went to our appointment and saw the baby and heard the heartbeat. We were on cloud nine! We couldn't wait to tell our family and friends, but we agreed we would wait until we were out of the first trimester.

When I had my first child, she was delivered at 35 weeks. Through that pregnancy we found out that my body doesn't produce progesterone, which is a crucial part of any pregnancy surviving. Due to this, I have to take progesterone injections every night, and I have to go in for weekly blood tests to monitor my levels. This also gives me the great little title of "high risk."

After one of my routine blood draws, the nurse called me while I was still at work. I knew the nurse well by this point, so I could tell by the tone of her voice that something was wrong. My heart immediately dropped. She explained to me that, even though I was on progesterone and that those levels looked great, my other levels had declined. She reassured me that sometimes this happens, and there was no need to worry because my numbers hadn't decreased tremendously, but enough to want to repeat the blood test.

I hung up and was upset, but I trusted God. In that moment I asked God to please allow His Will to be done, and to give me peace with whatever happens. If we lost this baby, I wanted it to glorify Him and somehow bring others to Him. At the same time, I begged and pleaded that He wouldn't use me as the person to do so. I wasn't sure if I was strong enough to go through the loss again.

My nurse called me after my second blood draw and said my doctor needed to talk to me. I knew what that meant. My doctor explained that all of my levels had dropped tremendously, and that he would need to do another D&C. He was very kind, loving, apologetic and reassuring. He told me he was on-call the next day and would like to schedule the D&C then. I said okay, but I was devastated. Not only had I just lost another baby, but the next day was my 25th birthday.

I called my husband and told him the news. Despite everything, my husband seemed so okay. He didn't seem upset, hurt, or angry. He definitely didn't act like he had just lost a baby! I, on the other hand, was inconsolable. What is wrong with me that I can't stay pregnant?

I called my mom and my mother-in-law to tell them, and I asked my mother-in-law to please check on my husband because he didn't show much emotion. I wanted to make sure he was actually okay, and not just putting on a brave front for me. My mother-in-law said, "Well Brooke, you didn't lose a real baby. You were only eight and a half weeks pregnant. That's not even a baby yet, so I'm sure he is fine."

I know she didn't mean any harm, and said it out of love and reassurance, but I was devastated by her words. How could anyone think that life growing inside a uterus, no matter how small, isn't a baby? She had a picture from our ultrasound on her fridge, yet she didn't see this as the loss of a baby? I was angry!

That night, my husband went above and beyond to celebrate my birthday a night early. We had an amazing night and I was at peace. The next day we woke up early to head to the hospital. My doctor greeted us in our room before the surgery and reassured us that he would take great care of me. He was very sympathetic and only ever referred to our baby as a baby.

Over the next few weeks and months, life went on for everyone, including my husband, but it stood still for me. I was hurting. My arms were empty and I just didn't understand why. My husband and I started trying again as soon as my doctor cleared us. During these months of negative tests, I developed a friendship and reliance on Jesus that was sweeter, richer, and deeper than I ever even thought possible this side of Heaven.

Two years later, my doctor came in on his off day to deliver our son. He not only came in on his off day, but he had to reschedule his family beach trip to the Bahamas so he could be there! One of the nurses was shocked to see him and asked him what in the world he was doing there. He glanced at me with a huge smile and grabbed my hand. He said, "Two years ago, I had to remove her baby who had quit breathing on her birthday. It was a horrible day for us both and she has hated her birthday ever since. I have the opportunity to make her birthday a happy day again, and I am honored she is allowing me to be here!" It was the most special delivery I could have ever dreamed of. There wasn't a dry eye in the room after we heard that first cry. In that moment, I felt God, and my miscarriages were worth it.

My children today know they have two siblings in Heaven, and that we will all get to be together one day. I still miss my babies and think of them often. I wonder what they would look like or whom they would act like. Would they like baseball? Would they want to take ballet?

When I sit and allow my mind to go crazy with these types of questions, I hear God telling me that they are with Him and not to worry because they are perfect. I must take care of my babies here. I am thankful that God allowed me to miscarry because, honestly, I don't think I would appreciate my pregnancies, births, or children as much as I do today had I never miscarried. I am thankful that God allowed me to miscarry, because I can now share with other women that He is the only one who can ever fill that hole in your heart from losing a child.

JULIE-ANN'S STORY

I believe our family was conceived in our hearts the night we rode the Cinderella Clydesdale horse-drawn carriage down the streets of old Decatur almost twenty years ago. My husband of less than two hours and I saw three beautiful girls peering through the window of a breathtaking Antebellum home. They ran out to meet us with sparkling eyes and excitement on their faces. My groom and I looked at each other and knew that this was a foreshadowing of our future. God was already preparing our hearts to receive our greatest blessings.

The road to those blessings, however, was fraught with struggle, heartache, tears, and more fear than I ever thought possible. Getting pregnant was challenging for us. I remember the heartache of being the only daughter-in-law without a grandchild to share for Christmases, birthdays, and other special family events. I felt left out and hurt at not being able to share in the sisterhood of being a mother. I felt like I would never be accepted into that family without producing a grandchild.

In the south, we are blessed with glimpses of warm days at the close of winter. I remember enjoying an afternoon run with the sun shining down, and feeling an intuition that there was life growing inside me. I waited with great anticipation to miss the first day of my period and take a pregnancy test, because I just knew it would be positive. I will never forget the joy that flooded my heart when the second line turned pink.

No sooner than that precious soul entered my life, it was taken away. I was completely heartbroken, but took that hurt to the feet of Jesus and allowed Him to heal me and give me a vision of that precious baby in Heaven reuniting spirits with Him in the mature form God created.

I was fortunate enough, after one cycle, to get pregnant again. I took test after test, just waiting for the second line to get darker. I was obsessed with knowing that my HCG level was increasing and even went in for blood work to see that it was doubling, as it should. My husband joined me for our first ultrasound at eight weeks as our doctor turned the screen away from us, had hushed conversations, laughter and smiles with the nurse, and then turned the screen back to us. Twins! Nervous and completely ecstatic were the best words to describe both of our emotions that day. I got phone calls from family members and my favorite brother-in-law even came to visit me at work. It was truly the very best of times.

The bleeding started the next week. I returned to the Ob/Gyn for an ultrasound to discover a sub chorionic hemorrhage that threatened the pregnancy. All I could do was be patient and pray. The bleeding continued, and when I went back for my 12 week appointment, I was no longer a twin mom, but the mom of a single baby. I was devastated. Hurt, anger, and disappointment were my closest companions for the rest of that pregnancy. I had fear, even after my beautiful daughter was born, that we would lose her still. A deep depression sank in.

With my two consecutive pregnancies, I had a sub chorionic hemorrhage each time and sat on pins and needles the entire first trimester. I was worried sick, but God was faithful to His promise to us that August night when our family of three precious girls was conceived in our hearts.

REFLECTION

By now you've seen that every single story is different. The paths to the present are seldom perfect. In fact, Jesus is the only person on Earth who walked a path of perfection. This experience is one that can be wrapped in hurt, disappointment, and fear, but we don't have to dwell there. Looking back, even through the devastation, each of these stories is a testament of God's faithfulness. Sometimes God isn't faithful in the way we might think, but He is faithful nonetheless.

ACTION

Take time today to reflect on the blessings in your life as well as the scriptures below. Write God's blessings down in your journal. God's love never fails (Psalm 136). Perfect love casts out all fear (1 John 4:18). Rest in knowing that His promise still stands. There are beautiful blessings to come.

DISCUSSION

1. We all have needs we are hoping and praying for, but it's refreshing to reflect on the things God has already done. Look at your list of blessings and add any "mountains" God has moved in your life. Let this "mountains moved" list be a reminder that He is FAITHFUL!

2. Now, what mountains are you still praying for Him to move? Read Mark 11:23 and Matthew 17:20. Reflect on these verses and write your "mountains to be moved" list in your journal. Now, lift your eyes above those mountains and look to the Lord (Psalm 121:1-2). Let Him be your helper!

Scripture

"I sought the LORD, and he answered me and delivered me from all my fears" (Psalm 34:4).

"There is no fear in love, but perfect love casts out fear. For fear has to do with punishment, and whoever fears has not been perfected in love" (1 John 4:18).

"For it is by grace you have been saved, through faith--and this is not from yourselves, it is the gift of God" (Ephesians 2:8).

CHAPTER 8: TOGETHERNESS
THREE STRANDS ARE STRONGER

*If it wasn't for my son, I wouldn't know
Jesus the way I do now... My baby
introduced me to Jesus firsthand.*

CRYSTAL'S STORY

I'll never forget being pregnant with our first baby. There I
was, focusing on perfecting the nursery and determined to
find cute baby boy clothes because everyone told me it was
difficult. I also kept thinking about how I wanted to get a
pillow monogrammed to rest behind me in the hospital to use
as a "backdrop" for those first pictures with our newborn
baby. I had it all planned out; or so I thought.

No one ever told me (or I failed to listen) that being pregnant
and having a baby didn't necessarily mean you'd go home
with a baby. It never, in a million years, crossed my mind that
anything like this could happen to me. Nothing could have
ever prepared me for the sudden and unexpected birth of our

first baby. He was born just a few weeks past the midpoint in a (normal) pregnancy—23 weeks, 4 days to be exact.

I remember being in the hospital the day after he was born and being so mad at myself over the things I had worried about before my precious tiny baby boy was born. I felt so stupid. It all seemed ridiculous, especially when my tiny 1.7-pound baby lay in an incubator fighting for his life. In the blink of an eye I learned what truly mattered in life. One of the many verses that came alive for me after the birth of my baby boy was Colossians 3:2: "Set your minds on things above, not on earthly things."

The morning after he was born, I vividly remember joining my husband in prayer as he was sitting in a chair. I, still in a hospital gown, got down on my knees on that cold hospital floor. I'll never forget how humble I felt coming to the Lord asking Him to spare our baby boy's life, yet praying for God's Will to be done. We knew God was ever so present, and had a great purpose in all He was doing through our son. Just as my husband and I had prayed together when we began trying to get pregnant, we prayed: "Your Will be done."

Through all of this we had peace; peace that surpassed all our understanding. Nothing in this entire world could have ever prepared us for what we witnessed and felt when our precious tiny baby boy went to be with Jesus just four days after he was born. We had never even held him, but even still, through God's love and power, I felt the pure joy any mom feels the first time she holds her newborn baby. I never held my baby alive, but holding my firstborn baby for the first time still filled me with an indescribable love. He was unbelievably perfect. I could have sat there in that chair and held him for eternity. Even with a broken heart, I have hope because I know that one day I WILL!

It's been almost four years, and I've come to realize that if it wasn't for my son, my precious tiny baby boy, I wouldn't know Jesus the way I do now. I would have never felt God and His love or seen Him work wonders the way I have since the birth and death of my son. My baby introduced me to Jesus firsthand.

Together, my husband and I leaned on each other and on God like never before. They were the only two who could understand my shattered heart. The only place I found comfort and rest for my weary heart and soul were with them.

Immediately after our loss, people began to inform me that there were "staggering statistics about how many couples don't survive the loss of a child." This couldn't be further from the truth for us. After all my husband and I experienced together, I had never felt so close to him. He was the hands and feet of Jesus as he cared for me and my every need, even through his own broken heart. I loved him when we were married, but this felt like *love*. This was the love we vowed to each other on our wedding day. We were truly living out our vows.

HALEY'S STORY CONTINUED...

They say hindsight is 20/20, and now I see how the enemy seeks to divide a marriage in seasons of hardship. Satan wasted no time pouncing on my marriage.

My husband was trying to comfort me, but my sorrow clouded my perception. It became hard to relate to him because I was constantly frustrated that he appeared to be uncaring. I concluded that he just didn't understand. He obviously didn't hurt the way I was hurting. We weren't experiencing the same thing. And he already had a child, my stepson, who had been wanting a little brother or sister. Since that baby hadn't come, I felt like I had let him down. I knew I shouldn't harbor resentment, but I couldn't help it. My feelings were putting miles between us with each passing day.

It was diving into scripture and prayer that finally convicted me. I was spending so much time judging my husband, that I hadn't stopped to try to understand him. I wasn't accepting him, as he was, where he was.

The truth is that people have different responses to loss and grief. He needed me just as much as I needed him. We said our wedding vows before God: "For better or for worse." It is easy to be loving in the "for better" times, but I was learning that it was during the "for worse" times that I must be intentional in my actions and filled with grace.

BRANDON'S STORY

I don't remember the exact day or time, unlike my wife, but I do remember the feeling when we found out that she was having a miscarriage. It was the first ultrasound appointment and we were hoping to hear and see a heartbeat. I can remember the pure joy I felt the first time I witnessed the heartbeat of our first child, and I was excited have that same experience again. This time was different.

I recall standing close to her as we smiled at each other and stared at the fuzzy black and white screen. Do you ever get that feeling in your gut, like something's not right? As soon as I saw the expression on our doctor's face shift, I felt it. I don't remember everything the doctor said, but I knew it wasn't the good news we had hoped for. Then, I looked at my wife. She looked completely broken and I had no idea what to do.

I remember trying to encourage her and saying we'd try again and that everything would be okay. It just wasn't God's plan, right? I could quickly tell that none of my words were going to make this situation better. She would say "I'm fine," but I knew in my heart that was not the case. I would ask, "What can I do to make it better?" but again her answer would be, "I'm fine."

As a man, I naturally want to fix things, and I wanted to "fix" this situation and make it better. No matter how hard I tried, no approach seemed to make her feel better. I knew my wife was hurting, and I felt completely helpless.

As the days and weeks went on, she "seemed" to be doing okay, but she wasn't, and I didn't really ask or talk about it anymore. I just assumed she would get over the miscarriage like some sickness or something. As you can imagine, this was a really bad assumption on my part. My lack of empathy, coupled with the pain, created a wedge in our marriage. I saw my wife's pain progress to anger as she said things like, "You probably wanted this to happen!"

How do you respond? Looking back, I think we both reacted rather than responded. She was filled with questions and anger, and I was just trying to put it behind us and pretend like it never happened. We were both handling the miscarriage in our own way, but neither of us in the *right* way. Rather than asking God to strengthen us and help heal us so we could use our story to help others, we became isolated from one another.

I became focused on work, and she found refuge in small groups. Although she found purpose through ministry, our lack of communication still widened the wedge in our marriage. The enemy loves to attack in isolation, and I truly believe we were under attack based on this weakness.

I'm not exactly sure when things got better for us, but I do know what steps we took to change. We realigned our priorities and began to trust the Lord. Trying to overcome a miscarriage in our own way was clearly not working for us. We both worked hard to reconnect to the Lord and let God work on our own hearts. We began to communicate with each other and worked through our healing and hurting together, rather than apart. God used this trial to bring us closer together and strengthen our marriage like never before.

We both worked hard to reconnect to the Lord and let God work on our own hearts. We began to communicate with each other and worked through our healing and hurting together, rather than apart. God used this trial to bring us closer together and strengthen our marriage like never before.

REFLECTION (FROM BRANDON)

We can all agree, at some point in our lives things don't go as planned: We don't get the job, we aren't getting pregnant, we received a bad report from the doctor, we lost a loved one, etc. At some point we will all be tested. It's difficult in midst of the trials and tragedy to consider them "pure joy." Things will happen to us and loved ones that we will never understand. I pray wholeheartedly for all those reading this book and those that are hurting right now. I pray that you will remain strong in your faith and trust God. God loves you, and He is always faithful!

ACTION

Lean in to the Lord. Ask for healing and how He can use you to help others. In addition to turning to God, turn to each other. Keep God at the center of your marriage, for a cord of three strands is not easily broken (Ecclesiastes 4:12). Don't give the enemy a stronghold (Ephesians 4:26-27)!

DISCUSSION

1. Look up the difference between a reaction and a response. Did you react to your loss or respond to it? What is the difference between the two?

2. Write down a list of your current priorities. Be honest. Where you spend most of your time and energy is where your priorities lie. How can you realign your priorities within your life to become closer to God?

3. Have you and your spouse been able to come together in unity as a result of your loss, or are you distancing yourselves from one another? What are some practical conversations you can have in order to come together (or to continue doing so, if you're already working on it)?

Scripture

"Be alert and of sober mind. Your enemy the devil prowls around like a roaring lion looking for someone to devour" (1 Peter 5:8).

"Don't sin by letting anger control you. Don't let the sun go down while you are still angry, for anger gives a foothold to the devil" (Ephesians 4:26-27).

"Consider it pure joy, my brothers and sisters, whenever you face trials of many kinds, because you know that the testing of your faith produces perseverance. Let perseverance finish its work so that you may be mature and complete, not lacking anything" (James 1:2-4).

"For the LORD is good and his love endures forever; his faithfulness continues through all generations" (Psalm 100:5).

CHAPTER 9: RELEASE THE WHY
BEAUTY FROM ASHES

I chose to let God use this pain to grow my faith in Him. It's easy to have faith when you know why or when you know the outcome. But when you are in the middle, and there are no answers, and you still don't know the end... that is when you find faith.

DANIELLE'S STORY

My story begins in the midst of a mess; one big, huge mess. Inside that mess was a mixture of pain, tears, laughter, joy, shame, guilt, and confusion. (Spoiler alert!) This is not how my story reads today. In this moment, there is hope, freedom, unconditional love, forgiveness, mercy, and clarity. Now that you know what chapter we are in now, allow me to rewind.

It was the fall of 2011. I was freshly divorced. Divorced for the second time in my short thirty years. Just when life looked bleak, I became reacquainted with an old friend. We were good friends when I was in high school and into my first years of college, but had lost touch. It had been over ten years since we had spoken, so when we reconnected, I thought that I was merely reuniting with an old friend. We were married six months later!

Because of a rocky medical history, I had accepted the fact that I may not be able to have children. But in March 2012, just two days after we got married, I took my first ever pregnancy test… It was positive!

We scheduled an appointment for an ultrasound, and we found out that I was around eight weeks pregnant. When I heard the heartbeat, it really started to sink in that I was going to be a mother.

Fast-forward to the night before Mother's Day of 2012. My very first Mother's Day as a mommy! I was a night shift nurse at the time. About an hour into my shift, I knew something was not right. I phoned the on-call OB doctor, and he said to walk over to have an ultrasound to make sure everything was okay. On the walk over, I called my husband. I told him that I didn't know what was going on, but I just felt like it was not good. He started getting ready so he could meet me at the hospital. He was over an hour away.

I arrived to the unit and they put me in a room. Very quickly, the doctor came in to check the baby and I out. He said everything looked great. My cervix was closed and there was no bleeding. He wanted to do an ultrasound just to make sure, but he felt like everything was okay. I called my husband and told him to stay home. I thought maybe it was just first time mommy jitters and nothing more.

The ultrasound technician was very polite. She made eye contact with me while we talked, but then her face changed. She stopped looking at me, and I immediately knew. I have been on that side as a healthcare professional. There is a look when we know something you don't know yet. When we know something that is going to completely change your life, as you know it. We try so hard to not have that look.

The nurse said she had to go talk to the Radiologist to make sure she had all the pictures she needed. She never looked at me again. I called my husband and told him it wasn't good. I cried, a lot. The doctor pulled a chair up next to my bed. His eyes were sad as he said, "Danielle, I do not have good news. We don't know why, but your baby's heart has stopped beating. It is possible that we just somehow can't see it. I am going to have you follow up with your doctor on Monday to have your testing repeated. We can see everything else, but we do not see or hear a heartbeat."

Just a few minutes after midnight, on my very first Mother's Day, I became a mother to an angel.

The remainder of the night was a blur. I went home and fell asleep. When I woke up, I had several text messages saying, "Happy Mother's Day!" They didn't know. We explained what had happened to our families and posted on Facebook that our little one no longer had a heartbeat.

I remember my husband and I just holding each other and crying. Why, God? Was this punishment because of my past?

Had I done something wrong? Why allow me to carry this child only to take it away? I was just fine thinking that I couldn't have children. I didn't ask for this, and now that I had it, it was gone. I was so angry. I was so confused. My heart ached in a way that I cannot even explain. We were ending the first trimester. It isn't supposed to happen this way!

Then, I realized I had to make a choice. I cried out to God. I thought of Jesus in the garden. I thought of how He had asked for this cup to be taken from Him. But then, God. Not my will, but Yours be done. I didn't need or want to know why. I knew my Father knew what I didn't. I knew He never got it wrong. I put my life, my family, and my Angel in His hands. I learned the true meaning of faith and hope during the days and weeks that followed.

I carried my Angel until Monday. My doctor completed many tests, and the result was no different. He talked to me for a long time. He told me I didn't do anything wrong. He said all the right things. Although he didn't intend it, his words still cut very deep. I would have to go through the process of "delivering" the tiny body that remained. The entire process would take over a month before my body began to heal. I had so many complications. When I thought about miscarriage, I thought about the emotional pain. I had never thought about the physical pain and changes that women go through on top of it. It is the worst thing I have ever experienced by far – physically, emotionally, and spiritually.

I adapted to the new normal. After a few weeks, I returned to work. Left foot. Right foot. We decided to leave the "nursery" empty. We just closed the door. It was almost like using that room for something else meant I was giving up hope. I knew now that I could get pregnant, and I prayed that God would bless us with another pregnancy. It might take a year, it might take five years, but the room would stay empty until then. Every time I looked at that room, I thought about our Angel.

Just a few months later, I wasn't feeling well and took a pregnancy test. It was positive! This time I was skeptical of those pink lines. If I was pregnant, it had to be very early, so my doctor told me to wait four weeks to come in for an ultrasound. We didn't tell anyone. I was convinced that it was something left behind from before.

Four weeks later, we learned that we were eight weeks pregnant again. That beautiful heartbeat. Again, I had to make a choice. I could live in fear; fear that it would happen again, fear that I wouldn't be able to handle it if it did. Or, I could walk in faith. I could ground myself with hope. I could walk in the power of knowing that my Father held me in His hands. I told God that I didn't have to understand how I got here. I didn't have to know the outcome to have peace in the middle. I already knew the end. In the end was hope. The one thing that could not be taken from me no matter the outcome.

My son was born in March of 2013, a year after seeing those lines that ended in sadness. I will never forget the pain and confusion, but I choose to remember it from a place of victory. I choose to celebrate the redemption and restoration. I choose to use my pain for God's purpose. I choose faith. I choose hope.

My prayer is that somewhere in this story, someone will find a glimmer of peace. If you are reading this, please know that you and your child(ren) are loved beyond all comprehension. I pray that you will know that this is not a punishment. I cannot tell you why; all I can tell you is that you will find strength and peace when you release the need to understand why.

I chose to let God use this pain to grow my faith in Him. It is easy to have faith when you know why, or when you know the outcome. But when you are in the middle, and there are no answers, and you still don't know the end…that is when you find faith. Real faith. Powerful faith. Faith the size of a mustard seed. Faith that moves mountains and sets God into motion in your life.

As I write this, I am in tears. My tears flow because I know the pain you have experienced. I know the sadness, confusion, and anger. I pray that you will allow God to take your pain and turn it into purpose. I pray He replaces the pain with promise. I ask God to overflow your heart with peace and clarity. I pray that you, too, will one day share your story of hope, faith, strength, and peace. As for me, my story is still not complete. I don't know what the chapters ahead will entail; all I know is how the story will end. Until then, I pray that God will continue to open avenues for me to share His light and love in even the darkest of places. The smallest hint of light will change your perception, even in the darkest of places.

WILLIE'S STORY

Instead of asking, "why me," I should ask Him "what's next," because God wouldn't allow any tribulation in our lives unless it could be used for our good.

My wife and I have known each other since middle school and started dating in high school. We got married in 2007, and in 2008 (after I got my master's degree), we moved to Tuscaloosa, Alabama. The next year we talked and sought God about having a child. We felt we were ready and wanted to share our hearts with a little bundle of joy.

In June, we celebrated Father's Day at our church. As fathers came forward to claim the gifts provided by the congregation, one of my fellow musicians slid me a note from my wife. Written on it were four words that would change my life forever… "Happy Father's Day, Daddy!"

I was breathless. Could it be that after many months of trying that I would become a father?! I ran to embrace my wife and made the announcement in front of the church. We rejoiced and thanked God for this life-changing blessing! We immediately set out to find a doctor. I told my family, friends, co-workers, EVERYONE! We made our appointments and I didn't miss a single one. I was on cloud nine! Nothing could bring us down.

Except the doctor's report… The first one was a little troubling, but not so much that we were overly worried. I continued to encourage my wife and assure her that everything was going to be all right. The next appointment was even less encouraging, and would prove to be the first real test of our faith.

My wife's pregnancy hormone levels had sharply decreased. We joined in prayer and continued to trust God that we were going to be parents. One day, my wife said she was concerned because she saw some spotting, so we made a visit to the hospital. Her regular doctor was on vacation, so we spoke to the on-call doctor. Despite the butterflies in my stomach, I still believed that we would receive good news.

Finally the doctor came in… I was NOT prepared for what he said next. There was virtually no detectable level of pregnancy hormone in my wife's system. The doctor flatly stated that we were having a miscarriage. I went numb. The doctor abruptly left the room and we sat there, dumbfounded… How could this have happened? We thought we had done everything right… vitamins, supplements, diet, and rest. We lived our lives according to God. What would we tell our family, friends, and co-workers?

Two weeks later the miscarriage was officially noted in the doctor's report. My wife took some time off to gather her thoughts and rest. I did the only thing I knew to do, pray and work…HARD.

The next few days were a blur. I felt as if I was living in a constant haze, drifting to work and back home. How could this happen? How could God let me down? What did I do wrong? I was working in Meridian, Mississippi, driving 200 miles every single day to keep food on the table after having been laid off from my previous construction job.

I wrestled against the enemy every day for weeks. Then, one morning as I was on my way to work, I heard the words "I'll Trust You" over the radio. I wept passionately as I told God "Even though I can't see my way through this, I'll trust you." When I got home I shared my experience with my wife, and to my amazement, she had heard the same song at the exact same time at the house! We rejoiced and prayed for unity.

Another morning, as I was reflecting in the shower, I felt the Holy Spirit saying "Why me or what next?" I asked God to reveal what it meant. Instead of asking, "why me," I should ask Him "what's next," because God wouldn't allow any tribulation in our lives unless it could be used for our good.

I quickly rushed into our bedroom and woke my still-sleeping wife to share God's revelation. The tears were streaming down her face as she received the encouragement. We knew God had not forgotten us. Furthermore, we knew NOTHING we had done caused the miscarriage. We stood on God's Word. NO WEAPON formed against us would prosper!

Empowered and encouraged, we began serving God like never before. In the midst of this storm, I accepted God's call to preach, and my wife started walking in her calling of evangelism.

On November 13, 2009, we celebrated my 27th birthday. I had just gotten off work and my wife was sitting in the living room. Before taking me to eat at my favorite restaurant, she wanted to give me a gift. It was a small paper bag. It was very

light, so I was thinking…CHA–CHING! (Gift card or
money!) But it was something EVEN better; inside the
bag was a baby bib with the words "I Love My Daddy."

Time seemed to stand still. Could it be true? Would I really
get the chance to be a dad again? I held my wife's hands and
wept, thanking God for His mercy.

We visited our doctor and started appointments again. In
December 2009, my wife and I heard our baby girl's heartbeat
for the first time. God answered our prayers! But He wasn't
through yet…

- The first time I found out I was going to be a dad –
  Father's Day 2009

- The day the miscarriage was noted in the doctor's
  report – July 16, 2009

- The day I found I was going to be a dad AGAIN –
  November 13, 2009

- The birthday of our daughter, Destiny – July 16, 2010
  (A year to the day we found out about the
  miscarriage!)

REFLECTION

It is natural to ask why, but don't dwell there. Ask God, "What's next?" Like the dandelion blows in the wind, ask God what seeds He wants you to sow. God knows your sorrow and will never forget you. As you sow your tears of sadness, you will reap in joy (Psalm 126:5-6). God's Word does not return void (Isaiah 55:11). Let your sorrow be part of your sanctification. All it takes is faith like a mustard seed (Matthew 17:20). God is not picking on you, He has HAND PICKED YOU! Do not give up on the promises of God. Your test is your testimony. His word says He will wipe every tear from our eyes (Revelation 21:4). There will be no more death, mourning, crying, or pain. Rejoice in the Lord and spread your seeds of hope.

ACTION

Read Psalm 56. In this psalm, David was going through a difficult time. The Philistines had captured him and he was a prisoner of war. He had reason to cry and be sorrowful, but in his sorrow he expressed his tremendous trust in God. David declares that God is for him (v. 9) and his trust overcomes fear (v. 11). In your journal, reflect on these verses and answer the discussion questions below. As you release the "why" and trust in the Lord, He will bestow a crown of beauty instead of ashes (Isaiah 61:3).

DISCUSSION

1. Are you asking God "Why me"… or are you asking Him "What next"? How is this affecting your relationship with Him? Take this time to ask God what seeds He wants you to sow.

2. As you read Psalm 56, what three things do you notice David mentions to overcome his fear? Are you afraid of what the future brings? How can you display thankfulness, trust, and praise in your life to overcome your fears?

Scripture

"But those who hope in the LORD will renew their strength. They will soar on wings like eagles; they will run and not grow weary, they will walk and not be faint" (Isaiah 40:31).

"Blessed is the man who remains steadfast under trial, for when he has stood the test he will receive the crown of life, which God has promised to those who love him" (James 1:12).

"But sanctify the Lord God in your hearts: and always be prepared to give an answer to everyone who asks you to give the reason for the hope that you have" (1 Peter 3:15).

"So is my word that goes out from my mouth: It will not return to me empty, but will accomplish what I desire and achieve the purpose for which I sent it" (Isaiah 55:11).

"That is why we never give up. Though our bodies are dying, our spirits are being renewed every day. For our present troubles are small and won't last very long. Yet they produce for us a glory that vastly outweighs them and will last forever! So we don't look at the troubles we can see now; rather, we fix our gaze on things that cannot be seen. For the things we see now will soon be gone, but the things we cannot see will last forever" (2 Corinthians 4: 16-18).

CHAPTER 10: CELEBRATE LIFE
Never Forgotten

I hope that you celebrate that baby's life as much as you celebrate the next, because no matter how short a life, all life deserves to be celebrated, and all loss should be mourned.

Emily's Story

I had to pee so badly, but they wouldn't let me go.
They said I needed a full bladder because it's easier to see the baby during the ultrasound. I remember feeling so frustrated, not only because of my full bladder, but because I had to fill out what seemed like fifty pages of paperwork before I *could* empty my bladder and see the baby I'd been waiting to see for eight weeks.

Finally, I was walked to the back room where I was greeted with a smile from everyone, because the happiness from carrying a baby is contagious. The ultrasound began and I saw the images right in front of me. My heart was beating out of my chest. This was exciting! This was a day my husband and I had been waiting for, for over a year.

But these images were different than the ones I'd seen on Facebook that all my girlfriends had posted. Something was wrong... I saw nothing because my body was just hours away from miscarrying.

The ultrasound tech was quiet, and I just knew. She left the room and my husband quickly assured me, "everything is fine." But don't tell that to a girl who has seen hundreds of ultrasound photos; that has searched Instagram for the hashtag "8weeks" to see what her baby should look like.

I knew it wasn't right. I remember being afraid to cry. I didn't feel as if I deserved to cry because "I wasn't that far along," and "this happens all the time." I remember holding back the tears with every ounce of my being, and not being able to look my husband in the face because I knew his pain would break me.

I was sent home to let my body naturally run its course, and it did. I felt everything but had nothing to show for it. My doctor didn't let me leave without warning, and she was right about everything. But what she didn't warn me about was everything that would happen after the initial heartbreak and pain.

She didn't tell me I was going to be reminded for weeks to come because my body was going to take that long to "clean out." She didn't tell me I was going to have to watch my husband weep. She didn't tell me how hard it was going to be to tell my mom what had happened. She didn't tell me that my body was going to continue thinking it was pregnant for weeks to come. She didn't tell me how hard it was going be to tell people I was fine when I wasn't. She didn't tell me that this was going to make me a jealous person overnight. She didn't tell me how much harder the question "When are you having kids?" was going to be. And she didn't tell me that it was going to be so hard losing someone I had never met.

But she *did* tell me it was okay to cry, and she did tell me that I wasn't alone.

Miscarriages are SO real and so common. In fact, one out of four women experience a miscarriage; but don't let that confuse you into thinking it hurts any less. As large as this statistic is, I still felt alone, and I have finally figured out why: because no one talks about it.

It wasn't until I started talking about it to my friends and family, that I slowly realized I *wasn't* alone. My mom, my aunt, my sister, and my sister's best friend have all experienced this heartbreak and pain; a heartbreak and pain I wouldn't wish upon my worst enemy.

People may wonder why I choose to talk about this after months have passed, but it's the harsh reality that time alone doesn't heal all wounds. I am hoping that sharing my story will help others with the healing process. I am not looking for pity, and I am not looking for answers. I am sharing this so that maybe one less woman will feel alone. I pray that this would be a reminder that there *is* hope after heartbreak.

This is my hope for you...

I hope that you won't feel alone.

I hope that you let yourself cry.

I hope that you will see the light at the end of the tunnel.

I hope that though your faith will be tested, you will be strong.

I hope you find peace.

I hope you won't be afraid to try again.

I hope that you don't blame yourself.

I hope that your friends hug you a little tighter.

I hope that you give someone else hope through your hardship.

I hope that you are a light in the darkest of times.

…and I hope that you celebrate that baby's life as much as you celebrate the next because no matter how short a life, all life deserves to be celebrated, and all loss should be mourned.

ERIN'S STORY

Until that day when we will meet our babies again, we will hold them in our hearts until we can hold them in Heaven.

This has been a journey of not only love, faith, hope and support, but also doubt, fear, anxiety, and jealousy. Through it all, I have thankfulness and joy.

My husband and I started down the path of building our very own family the day we exchanged vows. From the day I met him, I knew he was made to be a father. He had more love and faithfulness in his heart than any man I had ever met. He was an answer to a prayer that I had prayed since I was a little girl. I never wanted anything more than to be a mother. A mommy to a whole tribe of little ones, and I just knew he would be able to provide that life for me, for us.

After three short months of trying to conceive, we found out we were pregnant. Extremely overjoyed, we wasted no time planning for this child. I immediately collected all the baby items that my mom had saved for me to one-day use for my own children. We went ahead and took announcement photos, began refinishing my old baby furniture, and collected blankets that loved ones had made for us when we were born.

We really were living in bliss! Nobody warned us. Nobody told us about the statistics of miscarriage. We were two extremely healthy thirty year olds. We ate right, worked out, and took care of ourselves. And to top all that off, we had God on our side!

At eight weeks pregnant, we found ourselves in an emergency room being told by medical professionals that we had lost our baby. I think this was the only time in my entire life where I had no thoughts. My mind felt empty. My heart felt lonely. My body felt broken.

I questioned God. I mourned. But I'm also a fighter. We picked up the pieces and immediately started trying again. Two months later we found ourselves pregnant again. But this time, at three weeks, my body failed me again. We pressed on still. Exactly a year to the day that we lost our first, we also lost our third.

By this point we found a highly sought after fertility specialist. Friends and family had been encouraging us to find one. I was beyond apprehensive. God was our specialist! Through this entire year of pain, He was our rock. He was the one holding our marriage together in the face of so much adversity. I spent eight months being poked and prodded. Endless blood draws, hormone treatments, injections, medications, and uncomfortable tests as well as acupuncture, Chinese medicine, and crazy diets. It was scary to say the least. I questioned our path. If God really wanted us to have a baby, wouldn't He make that happen without all of this intervention? Was I really supposed to one day be a mommy?

We pleaded with God. I had family that didn't agree with the path we had taken. They never outwardly said it to us, but I could feel it in our conversations. Through all of this though, I had a peace in my heart. I knew God would never betray me. I knew that if I stayed positive and kept my eyes focused on Him, that He would provide. He was my strength.

On July 4, 2014, we conceived our fourth child through our second IUI. It was the picture-perfect pregnancy. With no complications, our son was born exactly a week early. God knew we couldn't wait another day to hold him in our arms. Our prayers had been answered!

Our story didn't end there though. Remember, I wanted a tribe! When our son was six months old we started trying again because we knew it could take a while. We prayed that this time we could conceive without any medical intervention. We tried on our own for six months with no luck. I made an appointment with our specialist and we headed down the same path. My goal this time...to give our son a sibling.

For the next seven months, we tried all the things that we credited for working the first time around, with no luck. We were told that our only option at this point would be IVF. We prayed hard and asked God to give us a peace about our next steps. We once again followed our hearts and pushed on. This time around though, we were not so silent. I began sharing our story on social media.

My thought process consisted of two things. First and foremost, I thought of all those women who were facing the same trials and tribulations. I knew how alone I felt the first time around. I never wanted anyone to feel that same pain. That same empty and broken feeling. I remember secretly scouring the web in the middle of the night in search for just one other woman that had a similar story; desperately searching for happy outcomes, but many times never finding much. It's such a personal journey that I totally understand why we hold it in. Second, by sharing our story, I also knew we would have a team of prayer warriors. A group of Jesus-loving, faithful people behind us.

Man, was I right. They came out of the woodworks! I started receiving messages from all over. Some of whom I knew, and others that I didn't. Messages of encouragement and prayer from women who were going through similar journeys, who just wanted someone to talk to. I shared it all. The good, the bad, and the ugly. It was a healing process for me, but it was also a public way to share my faith.

For the next few months, we endured a lot, but never gave up hope. We stayed the course with our IVF protocol. We made the controversial decision to have our embryos genetically tested (with the strong encouragement of our doctor and my desire to limit more miscarriages). By this point, I didn't know how much more loss I could mentally and emotionally endure. We sent nine embryos off to the lab for genetic testing. I will never forget that feeling. I felt like I had nine babies that I had just sent off to be scientifically studied for two weeks. To say it was hard would be an understatement.

I will also never forget the day they returned back to my doctor's office. I received the call from the head nurse. I answered the phone with extreme anticipation. It never really occurred to me that it might not be the most amazing news. At this point we were preparing ourselves for raising nine more babies. She informed me that seven of them would never survive outside the womb. All seven had multiple genetic disorders that most likely would end in miscarriage or die at birth. Talk about a gut punch.

I wanted nothing more than to celebrate the two healthy embryos that would hopefully one day be miracle stories. But I honestly felt like seven of my babies just died. You can call them embryos, you can call them fetuses, but they all are pieces of my husband and I. They are pieces of our hearts that were created in love, and I once again found myself mourning loss.

But how could I be so selfish? That's all that ran through my head. God has blessed us with a beautiful baby boy and two perfect embryos. So many women would be over the moon happy to have that, and I am beyond devastated.

I didn't have time. Everything with the IVF process is all about timing, and this time I didn't let myself heal. I didn't allow myself to understand and talk through it with God. A few weeks later we transferred the first embryo. I had no question that this would work! The doctors gave us great odds and we were positive that we would one day hold this child.

We got the positive pregnancy test, but immediately our numbers started dropping, and after a few weeks we learned that we had lost another baby. At this point all we could do was pray. We reevaluated, and my doctor threw everything but the kitchen sink at me. I was on every medication imaginable and I prayed day and night. I pleaded with God. This was our last shot! We couldn't afford another round of treatment and if I was being honest, I didn't know how much more my body could take.

A month later we tried for our final embryo transfer... I am happy to say we are expecting another baby boy in less than seven weeks. What did I learn through this process? Don't ever give up. Don't question God, because His timing is perfect. I may not get my whole tribe, but I have the most perfect family.

Dreams are just that. They are dreams. Stay positive and surround yourself with positive people. Even during some of the most difficult times in your own life, you can be a beacon of light for others. You will watch friends and family conceive and carry easily and jealousy will creep in. Don't let it! We are all children of God, and He has a plan for each of us.

With our son, we didn't know his gender until the day he was born. It was an awesome experience. I thought that was how I would want to have each of them. But after looking back at my first three miscarriages, I have always been a little sad that I couldn't put a gender to them. I never knew what to call them.

Some say science is way too invasive. But between science and God, I have one sweet boy on this Earth and another on the way. We decided it would help us heal and let go of the pain if we could know the sex of each of the eight embryos we lost. We celebrated with a balloon release. We sent eleven balloons to Heaven. I look up every day and know without a shadow of a doubt that we have five girls, three boys and three unknown tiny little guardian angels looking over us. Until that day when we will meet again, we will hold them in our hearts until we can hold them in Heaven.

REFLECTION

Just like loss should be grieved, life should be celebrated. It may be a one-time celebration, or something you commemorate each year. Whether it is a balloon floating up to Heaven, or an angel sitting on your mantle, it is healing to acknowledge and celebrate the life that was once inside of you. If you're still waiting on your promise, make room. When my sister-in-law and brother were experiencing a season of infertility, our aunt told them to pack a diaper bag as a demonstration of their faith in the Lord. My sister-in-law said it was a hard thing to do, walking in the baby aisle, picking out items, and allowing herself to believe it was going to happen, when her heart almost wanted to do the opposite to guard itself. "I was in such a low place when she gave me that advice. It was hard watching those around me get pregnant and have babies. Then, God put her in my path in that moment to point me towards Him. It was exactly what I needed." My sister-in-law said it was the first time she really and truly gave it to God. Contributors Emily and Danielle created a literal room in their homes. Emily said, "We aren't sure what the future holds, but we are hopeful. We know that HE hears the desires of our hearts and He WILL provide. Maybe in a month, maybe in five years, or maybe in a way we aren't expecting, but we have to live like we believe in His promises and not just say we do. So we are. I'm not saying there aren't days of grief and confusion, and there aren't hard days ahead, but I do believe this room will give me hope." Believe and you shall receive.

ACTION

Whether you release balloons, make something, purchase something, or display a reminder in your home, celebrate the memory of your baby/babies today. If you're still praying for God's promises, make room. Not just literally, but in your heart too. Pray and ask God to help you with any doubt and unbelief (Mark 9:23-24). Believe and you shall receive!

Father God, I come to You with a thankful heart full of joy and celebration for the lives that have been created in the midst of heartache. Lord, keep me from thinking that my baby's life was too short on earth to be celebrated. Your joy is my strength, and I thank You for taking care of my sweet baby in Heaven. As we celebrate in various ways on earth, I know that my child will have the ultimate gift of celebrating with You until we are reunited. Lord, reveal to me those in my life that I can confide in and celebrate these moments with. Show me how to be a blessing to others and a witness to You by celebrating the life that was within me. Remind my heart of your goodness by celebrating the promises of Your Word. May the joy and hope that You fill me with overflow. Allow me to see that You are a good good father every time I celebrate my precious baby. In Jesus' name I pray, Amen.

DISCUSSION

1. Do you believe that God will be faithful to you? Take some time to write out a prayer asking Him to help you believe and to make room for His promises in your heart. If you find yourself at a loss for words, use the prayer above as your guide.

2. Do you have a way to celebrate your child(ren) in Heaven? If not, what is something you could do to celebrate him/her?

3. Pick one of the scriptures below to memorize. Put it somewhere that you can see it and read it every day. BELIEVE in that scripture and in God's promises.

Scripture

"Truly I tell you," Jesus replied, "if you have faith and do not doubt, not only will you do what was done to the fig tree, but even if you say to this mountain, 'Be lifted up and thrown into the sea,' it will happen. If you believe, you will receive whatever you ask in prayer" (Matthew 21:21-22).

"Ask and it will be given to you; seek and you will find; knock and the door will be opened to you. For everyone who asks receives; the one who seeks finds; and to the one who knocks, the door will be opened" (Matthew 7:7-8).

"Truly I tell you, if anyone says to this mountain, 'Go, throw yourself into the sea,' and does not doubt in their heart but believes that what they say will happen, it will be done for them. Therefore I tell you, whatever you ask for in prayer, believe that you have received it, and it will be yours" (Mark 11:23-24).

CHAPTER 11: HOPE FOR TOMORROW
EVEN IF... IT IS WELL

I will never take for granted that week I was filled with hope, enthusiasm, and a freedom convinced that God had me on His mind all along.

SHEENA'S STORY

For almost four years we prayed for a child. Friends made bets to see how soon we'd get pregnant after being married. Family members who didn't understand infertility would comment on pictures asking my parents why they didn't have grandchildren yet.

We spent years in infertility treatments with no luck. Our clinic revealed that it would likely be impossible to conceive without assistance. We stopped going to the doctor, and I packed away the dream of having a child because it hurt too much. I rebuked the lie of the enemy that God was punishing me for my past sins, but I still wondered when my spirit was weak.

Sara Hagerty said it best… "I knew God was good, but was He good to me?" I asked Him to remind me of all the other ways He'd abundantly blessed our family. I didn't want the absence of a child to be the one thing I was holding against God when He had done so much for our family. I knew He was a big enough God to heal my womb, but wanted to know *why* He hadn't done that for me.

We started having discussions about whether or not to go back to the doctor or to pursue any calling for adoption. However, despite these discussions, there was a sense of peace within me that silently spoke to be expectant of God to provide a miracle.

During a time of fasting and prayer at our church in January 2016, God spoke to me through various women in my life. One of these vessels sat next to me in church one Sunday as I silently sobbed in my seat near the end of service. She said, "The Holy Spirit told me to tell you He has a miracle for you." Another said, "God wanted me to tell you that your baby isn't late." Other vessels came up to me earlier that year while I was pregnant (and didn't know yet) and said, "the Holy Spirit told me to pray for you…something is about to happen."

On April 12, 2016, I took a test on a whim, feeling confident it would be negative as it always had been in the past. However, a positive sign I had never seen before appeared in my hand! Convinced it was defective, I took another one. Another positive.

We were able to go to the doctor two days later, and my husband and I saw the flicker of a heartbeat. I saw a heartbeat within me that was not my own! Our nurse practitioner was so kind and spoke words of life over us as we received the confirmation that there was life within me. It was so hard to be excited at first, as fear overcame me. I confided in a few close friends to cover us in prayer, and excitedly purchased items we'd use in the coming weeks to tell our parents.

On the drive to our next doctor's visit a week later, a spirit of fear came over me that something could be wrong. My husband tried to convince me that I was worrying about nothing. Lying helpless on the exam room table during the follow-up ultrasound, I sat in silence as the technician stated that the doctor would explain everything on the monitor.

Though it hadn't happened yet, I was miscarrying. Four days later it finally happened in the middle of the night. My husband thought I was dying, and part of me felt like I truly was.

When I think back on those events, my mind doesn't think about the miscarriage. My mind and my spirit go back to that heartbeat. A covenant that God made with me that whether on Earth or in Heaven, the Lord made good on His promise that I would be a mommy. My mind and my spirit also go back to that week of hopefulness that I was able to experience being pregnant, filled with excitement about possibilities of my child's future. I also think back to how much peace and love and outpouring of care that was given by our church family.

Even if I am never to be an earthly mommy, I will never take for granted that week I was filled with hope, enthusiasm, and a freedom convinced that God had me on His mind all along. It is part of my own sanctification journey that I continue to live with the same level of joy and hope that He gave me during that blessed week of promise and life within me. He made good on His promise that He would show me a miracle...show me a sign that life is possible within me.

Though it has been over a year since our miracle pregnancy and miscarriage, I continue to ask God to remind me of His goodness and reveal His plans. My heart is at a peace, a peace that only He can provide. But there are days that my spirit is weak and doubt creeps in.

Reading a book recently written by my pastor, I was prompted to look up the meaning of my name. Although I knew my parents named me after a character from a popular movie the year of my birth, I still lingered with curiosity about the true meaning of my name *outside* of pop culture.

Tears ran down my face as I saw that the Hebrew translation of Sheena means, "God is gracious" and "God's gift." All of this time I had wondered about God's goodness to me. Before He formed me in the womb, He knew me. Before my parents named me, God had already given me a name. Though God may work in mysterious ways, His heart is an open book. I know He has been gracious to me according to His sovereign will.

Even if I am never to be an earthly mommy,
I will never take for granted that week I was
filled with hope, enthusiasm, and a freedom
convinced that God had me on His mind all
along.

"And if not…He is still good" (Daniel 3:18).

THE FINAL CHAPTER
(HEATHER'S STORY TO BE CONTINUED…)

As I sit here putting the finishing touches on this book, I am writing a chapter that I never wanted to write… Lines that faded as soon as they came.

Looking back in my prayer journal the day I got a positive test, I wrote, "I am so excited! I trust you Lord and praise you for this joy."

From the very beginning, I had my doubts. Just like the time before, the lines weren't getting darker. I Googled every single symptom and checked my pregnancy tracker app religiously. I was looking for any confirmation that things were all right to release the fear. I was looking in the *wrong* place.

Every year our church holds a women's conference, and this year the timing couldn't have been more perfect. All I could do was smile when I saw the theme for the event… "Without Fear." The logo even had plus signs! It was as if God was speaking directly to me.

At the beginning of the conference I sobbed during every song. The fear was debilitating. I was frozen by the reality of what could happen. By the end, my tears were different. They were joyful. I felt like I had given my fear to God. My next journal entry declared, "I put this in God's hands and know, that regardless the outcome, He has a purpose and a plan."

Feeling more brokenhearted than hopeful, I had to release my frustrations to God. The Sunday after it happened, I didn't sing one single word at church. I couldn't bring myself to sing of God's faithfulness when it felt like maybe His faithfulness wasn't for me.

Then, the message. (Don't you just love when God does that?) It stepped on my toes, but in the best way. It was about humility. In that moment I realized that I was living in a place of heartbreak, wondering "why me," when in reality God wants us to live in a place of humility. I don't know why God's not answering my prayers in the way that I would like, but I do know it's not about me. Faithfulness is not a feeling; it's a choice you can make, even in the midst of frustration.

In that week that I saw positive lines, I had an experience with God at the conference, and had joy hosting a baby shower in my home, that I wouldn't have had otherwise. I had prayed to God for motivation to make the two-year dream for this book a reality. Something had been holding me back from finishing, but now I know why.

The minute the nurse hung up the phone after telling me my levels were too low, although I was heartbroken, I knew my prayer had been answered. Our ministry that had grown quiet had new life. God confirmed His purpose, and I had to surrender my plans, once again.

I have needed every single word on these pages as much as anyone else. I have hope and motivation to pursue my calling greater than ever before. As I have started writing again, and have watched others bravely share their stories, I have realized that God IS faithful. Maybe not in the way my heart desires, but I trust that *His* plan is greater.

Instead of asking, "Why me?" I will praise God and surrender saying, "Use me." His arms are open, and I will come running. Better yet, I'll kneel to the ground in humility, because as our pastor shared, you can't fall from face down. It is from that lowly position that God will lift me up.

REFLECTION

As much as I would like to tell you that you have a baby on Earth in your future, I can't. That is between you and God. What I *can* tell you is that GOD IS FAITHFUL. I pray that you develop an unshakeable faith and relationship with Him where you're able to say, "even if, He is still good." Rest in your soul that it is well. God's got you, sweet sister. You have a purpose to be a light that shines bright. There will be hard days, but you have hope. Hope for an eternal life with the Lord. You'll rock your sweet babies for eternity in Heaven. Take heart in this hope and share it with the world.

ACTION

Our prayer for this book is that it would bring healing and hope for those that need it most, through faith in Jesus Christ. Let this book be just a step in your journey to draw closer to the Lord. Don't stop now! Whether it's through sharing your story, celebrating your baby/babies, or passing this book along to someone who is currently experiencing loss, please share your hope for tomorrow!

DISCUSSION

1. Sara Hagerty said, "I knew God was good, but was He good to me?" Do you find yourself thinking this sometimes? What types of feelings/emotions does this statement invoke?

2. Read Daniel 3:18. In what ways does this verse speak to you?

3. Can you truly tell God to "Use me" in complete humility and surrender? If not, take some time to pray to God and ask Him to help you surrender.

Scripture

"Humble yourselves before the Lord, and he will lift you up" (James 4:10).

"Rejoice at all times. Pray without ceasing. Give thanks in all circumstances; for this is God's will for you in Christ Jesus" (1 Thessalonians 5:16-18).

"Praise be to the God and Father of our Lord Jesus Christ, the Father of compassion and the God of all comfort, who comforts us in all our troubles, so that we can comfort those in any trouble with the comfort we ourselves receive from God. For just as we share abundantly in the sufferings of Christ, so also our comfort abounds through Christ" (2 Corinthians 1:3-5).

"May the God of hope fill you with all joy and peace as you trust in him, so that you may overflow with hope by the power of the Holy Spirit" (Romans 15:13).

ACKNOWLEDGEMENTS

Thank you to my amazing husband who supports me in every endeavor and is my very best friend. Your contribution to this book, with the exception of our daughter, is the greatest gift you've ever given me.

To our beautiful blessing Brinley who makes the world a brighter place everyday. May you always "spread your joy" and keep Jesus at the center of your heart. I love you to the moon and back to Alabama, with all my heart and every beat.

Thank you to the women (and men) who were willing to share their stories for this book. May God bless you for opening your hearts to help others.

Thank you to our churches, families and friends who helped us find hope and held us up through the heartache.

Special acknowledgement to my freedom small group sisters, women of Church of the Highlands, and family and friends who have prayed for me and encouraged me along the way. And to the women of Craving God Ministries for your dedication, inspiration, support and faithfulness.

Thank you to my sister-in-law turned sister-in-love to downright sister, Tiffany, for tirelessly editing this book as the lead editor to make it the best version possible. You are the best friend and sister I never had but always wanted.

To the rest of the editing team (Dani, Caitlin, Victoria, Jessica, Heather, Brittany, and Sheena), thank you so much for being such an integral part of this book. Your contributions have been amazing. You are rock stars for making the impossible possible!

MOST importantly, praise God who works all things for good and through His son Jesus provides salvation, the true source of hope.

ABOUT THE AUTHOR

HEATHER SHIPLEY is a former marketing professional turned college instructor with a passion for writing, speaking and sharing hope in God's Word in order to encourage women to find freedom and live the abundant life God intended. She is an alumna of the University of Alabama who lives in Tuscaloosa with her husband and 5-year-old daughter.

In January 2016 she founded Craving God Ministries as a platform to give women a voice. She believes that God has given each of us talents that should be used for His glory (1 Peter 4:10). The Craving God Ministries platform can be summed up with a simple question: "What do you crave most?" The goal is to provide encouragement through transparent testimonies and truth in the word to ignite passion and relationship so readers can answer that question with the one thing that matters most, God.

Collectively, the Craving God Contributors come from diverse professional backgrounds and write/speak from personal experience on most things women today face including miscarriage, infertility, adoption, loss, marriage, parenting, body-image, leadership and more.

For more information visit <u>CravingGod.com</u>.

CAN WE ASK A FAVOR?

If you enjoyed this devotional book from Craving God Ministries, and found it useful, can we ask that you provide a short review on Amazon? We do read all the reviews personally so that we can continually write what our readers are wanting.

Also, as you're reading, please feel free to engage with us on social media using the hashtag #BrokenheartedHope. You can find Craving God Ministries on Facebook, Instagram and Twitter. We'd love to see pictures of you enjoying the book or hear about key takeaways from each chapter!

And of course, we would love to hear your story and pray for you specifically during this journey. We have guests on our blog each week and would love to invite you to share your story there as well. Contact us on our website or email heather@cravinggod.com.

Thank you so much for your support!